. THE ULTIMATE .

NEW MOM'S COOKBOOK

A COMPLETE FOOD AND NUTRITION RESOURCE
FOR EXPECTANT MOTHERS, BABIES AND TODDLERS

AURORA SATLER

WITH ALLISON CHILDRESS, PHD, RDN, LD

PAGE STREET
PUBLISHING CO.

PAGE STREET
PUBLISHING CO.

FOR JOSH, JACK AND LILA

CONTENTS

Introduction / 9

PREGNANCY FOODS / 11

Bun in the Oven Banana Zucchini Bread / 12

Happy Tummy Gingery Lemonade / 15

Creamy Lemon Comfort Rice / 16

Mom's Cure-All Chicken Noodle Soup / 19

Don't-Need-No-Deli-Meat Chicken Salad Sandwich / 20

Truffle Parmesan Crack Fries / 23

I ♥ Peanut Butter Chicken Skewers / 24

Baby Needs Pizza Home-Baked Remedy / 27

Full-Term Twice-Baked Potatoes / 28

Prego Picnic Chili Lime Fruit Cones / 31

Tropical Tummy Mango Faux-'Jito / 32

Strawberry "Margarita" for Mamas / 35

Baby Shower "Sangria" / 36

Foods to Avoid When Expecting / 38

Foods to Limit When Expecting / 39

Food Safety / 40

Gestational Diabetes / 41

GETTING READY FOR BABY / 43

Home-Baked Granola / 44

Make Ahead, Enjoy Later Pancake Mix / 47

Blueberry Buttermilk Pancakes / 48

Freeze-by-the-Batch Tomato Sauce / 51

Dinner-in-a-Pinch Classic Pesto / 52

Freezer-Friendly Chicken Chile Enchiladas / 55

Mom-to-Be Sausage and Veggie Ziti / 56

Black Bean and Quinoa Burgers / 59

Fork-Free Turkey and Mushroom Hand Pies / 60

40-Weeks-and-Counting Spicy Eggplant Parmesan / 63

Baby's Eviction Notice Pineapple
Teriyaki Chicken Stir-Fry / 64

Tips and Myths on Speeding Delivery
After 40 Weeks / 66

Dates for Your Third Trimester / 66

Building Your Pantry / 67

BREASTFEEDING FOODS / 69

Goddess Dressing with Crudités / 70

Calcium-Rich Whipped Feta Dip / 73

Mama's Guacamole / 74

Home-Style Salsa / 75

Gotta Rehydrate Cucumber Tomato Salad / 76

Orzo and Sundried Tomato Salad / 79

Grab-and-Go Green Pasta Salad / 80

Quick-Fix Tofu and Kale Stir-Fry / 83

So-Easy-It's-Sinful Rice and Bean Bowls / 84

Soba Noodle and Broccoli Rabe Buddha Bowl / 87

Alcohol and Breastfeeding / 88

Nutrition for a Breastfeeding Mother / 88

Breastfeeding Resources / 89

FIRST FOODS (4 TO 6 MONTHS) PLUS RECIPES FOR USING LEFTOVER PUREES/ 91

First Foods Timeline / 92

Introducing Solids: Myths and Facts / 93

Food Safety for Infants / 94

Equipment for Starting Solids / 94

No-Cook First Foods / 95

Grandma's Effortless Applesauce / 96

Apple, Carrot and Ginger Muffins / 99

Pear Puree / 100

Pear and Oat Smoothie / 103

Butternut Squash Puree / 104

Butternut Squash Mac 'n' Cheese / 107

Carrot Puree / 108

Carrot Cumin Soup / 111

Sweet Potato Puree / 112

Southwest Sweet Potato Cakes and Black Bean Salsa Fresca / 115

Mango Puree / 116

Mango Sorbet / 119

The Dirty Dozen and Clean 15 / 120

Portion Sizes for Babies and Toddlers / 121

Tips for Cooking with and Feeding a 6-Month-Old / 121

COMBINATION FOODS (6 TO 8 MONTHS) / 123

Introducing Water / 123

Baby Guacamole / 124

Apple, Sweet Potato and Corn Puree / 127

Pear, Kiwi and Spinach Puree / 128

Pumpkin, Apple and Carrot Puree / 131

Very Berry Puree / 132

Very Berry Coconut Popsicles / 135

Pea, Potato and Leek Puree / 136

Pea, Potato and Leek Soup / 139

Creamed Corn and Chicken Casserole / 140

Food Allergies / 142

Tips for Picky Eaters / 142

EXPANDING TASTES (8 TO 10 MONTHS) / 145

Introducing Dairy / 146

Stop and Go Foods / 146

Very Berry Oatmeal Breakfast / 148

Banana Rice Pudding / 151

White Bean, Pumpkin and Kale Puree / 152

Munchkin's Fried Rice / 155

Rinkles' Risotto / 156

Salmon and Sweet Potato Puree / 159

Winner Winner Chicken Dinner / 160

Little Shepherd's Pie / 163

Meat Textures Tots Like / 164

Finger Foods for Travel / 164

Babyproofing the Kitchen / 165

FAMILY MEALS (12 MONTHS AND UP) / 167

Mommy and Me Green Smoothies / 168

Small Bites Mini Quiche / 171

Baked Eggs Brunch for the Sleep Deprived / 172

Minestrone Soup with Ditalini / 175

Cut the Carbs Chicken Lettuce Wraps / 176

Chicken Pita Sandwiches / 179

Goat Cheese and Roasted Veggie Tart / 180

4 Bean Vegetarian Chili / 183

3 Cheese Chile Cornbread / 184

Cloudy Day Meatballs / 185

Heart-Healthy Mussels / 189

Butternut Squash and Chickpea Curry in a Hurry / 190

Everything-but-the-Kitchen-Sink Frittata / 193

Tender Turkey Meatloaf / 194

Friday Night Roast Rosemary Chicken / 197

Sinfully Succulent Skirt Steak and Mango Salad / 198

It's OK Not to Share Jerk Chicken Sandwiches / 201

Our Favorite Fish Tacos / 203

One-Pot Shrimp and Creamy Peanut Noodles with Hidden Veggies / 206

I Can Pretend It's Date Night Gnocchi / 209

Creamy Curry Chicken Penne / 210

Impressively Easy Rolled Hanger Steak with Goat Cheese and Spinach / 213

Bixby's Liquid Fire Brisket / 214

Brisket Sliders with Carrot Cilantro Slaw / 217

Brisket Tacos / 218

Acknowledgments / 220

About the Authors / 221

Index / 222

INTRODUCTION

I set out to write this cookbook both as a mom and as a chef. As a mom, I know how crucial nutrition is to a growing child, and as a personal chef, I am passionate about making those first experiences with food good ones.

A new baby brings so many changes to a home. This cookbook aims to ease all those transitions with simple meals and easy-to-digest nutritional information for each stage. The purpose of this book is also to feed the entire family. Often baby cookbooks are purchased with the best intentions and forgotten as soon as a child moves beyond purees. There is no reason for parents to starve while feeding their infant a rainbow palate of homemade food. In this cookbook, you'll find recipes from day one of your pregnancy to family meals that will last you well into the toddler years. On top of all the delicious purees, there are recipes for mocktails, addictive appetizers to satisfy the most intense pregnancy cravings, one-dish family meals to feed everyone in one fell swoop and "date night in" meals for parents in need of a culinary escape.

Nutrition begins in the womb and healthy habits are passed down from the parents. That's why making home-cooked meals and eating together as a family are so important. This book will set the foundation for your child to be a healthy eater who enjoys a wide variety of foods right from the start.

Food is something you worry a lot about with your first child. There are so many dos and don'ts when it comes to eating during pregnancy, and you'll hear voices—often those of strangers—warning you about the dire consequences of some ingredient you had never thought twice about. If you're breastfeeding, you'll worry if your child is latching well and gaining enough weight, and then as they get teeth, you'll worry if your child is going to bite you. As you introduce solids, you'll stress about allergies, whether your child will be a picky eater, if your child is getting enough iron, vegetables, protein, vitamins, calories, love—you name it!

In writing this book, I wanted to make the process of introducing solids as painless and fun as possible. I also know how important it is to work with a nutritionist, and what a great gift Allison's contributions have been to this book. I relied on her professional expertise for all the nutritional information that fills this cookbook. With all that comes from being a new parent you don't have the time to tack on getting your PhD in the process. Trust me, I didn't. That's why I turned to Allison, who added wonderful insights as well as her own wicked sense of humor as a fellow mom. Knowing that you have a professional on your side takes away so much of the worry that you have as a first-time parent.

A good cookbook also shouldn't feel like homework. It should be helpful and dog-eared and food stained from years of loving use. My hope for this book is that it will be as worn and stained as a child's favorite toy; that it will help new families just starting out and give inspiration to families who are in a meal rut. And most importantly, I hope it nourishes those you love most.

PREGNANCY FOODS

When you're pregnant, you don't have the same relationship with food you had before your pregnancy. It either turns your stomach or consumes your thoughts with intense and specific cravings. Since this journey begins with pregnancy, I knew pregnancy foods would be a crucial chapter in recipe development.

A mother begins nourishing her baby right in the womb. These recipes set out to ease those upset stomachs, satisfy those cravings and indulge in some fun for the celebrations that come with welcoming a baby into the family.

BUN IN THE OVEN
BANANA ZUCCHINI BREAD

MAKES 1 LOAF

This is an easy-to-digest breakfast that is tummy friendly and full of goodness. Many baked goods contain eggs, which are high in choline. Choline is a B vitamin, and you need 450 mg of choline per day during pregnancy. Many prenatal vitamins have no choline at all.

This is also toddler approved, great for using up bananas that are about to become overripe and has the bonus of combining two great loaves into one healthy and totally delicious recipe.

6 tbsp (85 g) butter

½ cup (100 g) brown sugar, packed

1 egg

1½ cups (345 g) mashed bananas (3 ripe bananas)

1 cup (175 g) grated zucchini (about 1 small zucchini)

1¼ cups (156 g) all-purpose flour

½ cup (45 g) oats

¾ tsp baking soda

¼ tsp salt

Preheat your oven to 350°F (177°C).

Grease a 5 × 9-inch (12.7 × 23-cm) loaf pan.

In a large bowl, cream the butter and sugar with an electric beater. Next, add the egg and mix well. Mix in the banana and zucchini.

In a medium bowl, whisk the flour, oats, baking soda and salt to combine. Slowly add the flour mixture into the wet ingredients, stirring until just mixed.

Pour the batter into the loaf pan and bake in the center of the oven for about 60 minutes. Test with a wooden toothpick or skewer; once it comes out clean your bread is ready. Allow to cool for 10 minutes before removing from the pan to finish cooling on a wire rack.

NOTE: This bread lasts about 2 days out on the counter under plastic wrap or in a sealed plastic container and up to a week refrigerated. Be sure to cool completely before storing. In hot weather, watch it more diligently and keep in a cool, dry place.

HAPPY TUMMY GINGERY LEMONADE

SERVES 4 TO 5

You don't have to be suffering waves of nausea to enjoy this drink. It is soothing and refreshing all at once with the bonus of having all the aromas that calm a queasy stomach. If you're worried about your sugar intake, you can increase the amount of water. Serve this drink over a glass filled with ice cubes and add a fun straw to trick yourself into thinking you're having a cocktail!

GINGER SIMPLE SYRUP

1 cup (200 g) sugar

1 cup (237 ml) water

¼ cup (24 g) sliced ginger

LEMONADE

1 cup (237 ml) lemon juice (from about 8 lemons)

1 cup (237 ml) ginger simple syrup

2½ cups (592 ml) water

TO MAKE THE GINGER SIMPLE SYRUP

In a medium stockpot, simmer the sugar with the water until dissolved. Add the ginger and bring to a boil. Reduce to a simmer and cook for 10 minutes. Allow to cool, then remove the sliced ginger.

TO MAKE THE LEMONADE

In a large pitcher, mix together the lemon juice, syrup and water. Refrigerate. When ready to serve, pour over ice.

CREAMY LEMON COMFORT RICE

MAKES 3¾ CUPS (698 G)

For mamas-to-be who need more sustenance than saltines and ginger ale, this definitely fits the bill. It is also a wonderful comfort for anyone with an upset tummy or sore throat.

3 tbsp (43 g) butter, divided

½ cup (76 g) finely chopped sweet onion

1 clove garlic, minced

½ tsp dried thyme

1¼ cups (263 g) jasmine rice

2½ cups (592 ml) chicken stock

1 tsp lemon juice

Zest of ½ lemon

½ tsp salt

In a medium sauté pan with a lid, add 2 tablespoons (29 g) of butter and the sweet onion. Sauté for about 4 minutes on medium-high heat until the onion is translucent. Add the garlic, thyme and rice, and sauté for 3 minutes, stirring constantly.

Add the stock, juice, zest and salt. Bring the mixture to a boil, then cover and reduce to a simmer for 18 minutes.

Fluff and mix in the remaining butter before serving.

MOM'S CURE-ALL CHICKEN NOODLE SOUP

SERVES 6

Broth is the key to a good chicken noodle soup. The more time you invest in making an ultrarich base, the better and more therapeutic this soup feels. For the best broth you need bones, so whenever I roast a chicken (frequently), I always save the bones.

This soup has the magical mom powers of curing what ails you. It is a meal that goes easy on a turbulent stomach and also gets you through cold and flu season with enjoyable ease.

THE ULTIMATE CHICKEN BROTH

1 whole chicken carcass (after roasting), skin removed

2 sweet potatoes, peeled and quartered

2 carrots, peeled and quartered

1 large sweet onion, peeled and quartered

2 sprigs rosemary

2 cloves garlic

2 (32-oz [946-ml]) cartons chicken stock

2 cups (473 ml) water

CHICKEN NOODLE SOUP

10 cups (2.5 L) ultimate chicken broth

1½ cups (183 g) thinly sliced carrots

1½ cups (152 g) thinly sliced celery

1 cup (150 g) frozen peas

2 cups (280 g) diced cooked chicken breast

2 cups (320 g) cooked egg noodles

Sea salt and freshly cracked pepper

TO MAKE THE ULTIMATE CHICKEN BROTH

In a large stockpot, add the chicken, sweet potatoes, carrots, sweet onion, rosemary and garlic, and cover with the chicken stock. Add the water, then bring to a boil. Once boiling, reduce to a medium simmer. Simmer covered for at least 20 minutes and up to 2½ hours (it gets better with time).

After the mixture has cooked, lay a large bowl in the sink and put a colander inside the bowl. Strain your broth through the colander. You want to shake the colander to get all the broth as well as some of the cooked potato and carrots. Discard the bones, onion, rosemary, garlic and any vegetables that remain in the colander.

This makes an incredibly thick and rich broth. It is liquid gold.

TO MAKE THE CHICKEN NOODLE SOUP

In a large stockpot, bring the broth to a boil, covering with a lid as you do. Once boiling, add the carrots and celery. Cook for 10 to 12 minutes until soft. Add the peas and cook for 2 minutes, then turn off the heat and add the chicken and noodles. Cook for 2 minutes until warmed, then season to taste with salt and pepper.

NOTE: Substitute whole grain noodles to make this a great meal if you suffer from gestational diabetes.

DON'T-NEED-NO-DELI-MEAT CHICKEN SALAD SANDWICH

SERVES 4

When you want a great cold sandwich but need to steer clear of the deli aisle, this one fits the bill. With both chicken and Greek yogurt, this recipe is packed with protein. During pregnancy, your protein intake needs to increase, so devour your sandwich with glee knowing you're getting the right nutrition for you and your baby!

This is also a great option for toddler lunches. Just remove the nuts from the recipe and make sure the celery is cut superfine.

1 tbsp (15 ml) olive oil

1 lb (454 g) chicken breasts (tenders)

Sea salt and freshly cracked pepper

¼ cup (59 ml) Greek yogurt

¼ cup (59 ml) mayonnaise

½ tsp Dijon mustard

2 tbsp (4 g) freshly chopped tarragon

¼ cup (30 g) diced pecans

¼ cup (25 g) thinly sliced celery

¼ cup (31 g) dried cranberries

Whole grain bread or rolls for serving as a sandwich, optional

In a large frying pan, add your olive oil and heat for 1 minute. Season your chicken generously with salt and pepper. Add the chicken breasts and cook for about 4 minutes per side on medium-high heat until cooked through and no longer pink. Rest the chicken breasts on a large plate for 4 minutes so they can retain their juices. Once cool, dice the chicken. Move the diced chicken to a large bowl and make sure to add any juices that dripped onto the resting plate, pan or carving board.

Mix the Greek yogurt, mayonnaise and mustard with the chicken. Then add the tarragon, pecans, celery and cranberries, mixing until everything is combined. Season once more to taste with salt and pepper. Serve on whole grain bread or rolls as a sandwich or simply enjoy as is.

TRUFFLE PARMESAN CRACK FRIES

SERVES 4 (OR 2 PREGNANT WOMEN)

These are called crack fries for a reason. Homemade french fries like these are so mind-blowingly good it's downright criminal. But you don't have to feel too guilty about gobbling these up because potatoes are packed with potassium, which can help get rid of those nighttime leg cramps. Talk about a tasty bonus!

PARMESAN GREMOLATA

1 cup (60 g) fresh parsley leaves, finely chopped

1 clove garlic, finely minced

Zest of 1 lemon

3 tbsp (34 g) grated Parmesan cheese

FRIES

6 medium-sized Yukon Gold potatoes

Canola or vegetable oil for frying (about 6 cups [1 L])

Sea salt

Truffle oil for drizzling

TO MAKE PARMESAN GREMOLATA

Mix the parsley, garlic, lemon zest and Parmesan cheese in a small bowl until well blended. Set aside until your fries are ready.

TO MAKE THE FRIES

Scrub your potatoes thoroughly. Lay out a baking sheet with paper towels covering it. Cut your potatoes into ¼-inch (0.5-cm)-wide matchsticks (french fry–size). You don't need to peel your potatoes; a little of the skin gives them a nice rustic look. Place the cut potatoes on the paper towel–lined baking sheet and rub off any moisture. Dump the potatoes in a large Dutch oven and cover them with the oil. You want the oil to just cover the mound of fries.

Cover the Dutch oven with a splatter guard and bring the oil to a boil. Heat for 30 to 35 minutes without stirring until your fries are crispy and golden brown. Scoop out the fries with a spider or large slotted spoon and lay them in a single layer along the paper towel–lined baking sheet. Immediately season the fries generously with sea salt. Then drizzle with the truffle oil and sprinkle with the gremolata to your liking. In my house we use the seasoning term *generously* very, well, generously. Go big or go home!

These fries are best enjoyed right after frying, but if you find yourself with leftovers, you can freeze and reheat them.

NOTE: For just a hint of truffle flavor you don't have to buy 100 percent pure truffle oil. You can often find a cheaper alternative that is a blend or a truffle-infused oil. A little bit of flavor goes a long way.

I ♥ PEANUT BUTTER CHICKEN SKEWERS

SERVES 2 TO 3

Peanut butter and pregnancy go together like peas and carrots. These chicken skewers definitely satisfy that specific craving. They also make a great appetizer if you intend to share, though there's no shame in keeping them all to yourself.

PEANUT SAUCE

1 lime, juiced

2 cloves garlic, minced

1 tbsp (15 g) minced ginger

1 tbsp (15 ml) sambal

2 tbsp (30 ml) hoisin sauce

3 tbsp (45 ml) soy sauce

3 tbsp (34 g) peanut butter

1 tbsp (15 ml) honey

SKEWERS

1½ lbs (680 g) chicken breast, cut into 1 × 1-inch (2.5 × 2.5-cm) cubes

4 scallions, sliced for garnish

Preheat the broiler to high.

TO MAKE THE PEANUT SAUCE
In a medium bowl, mix together the lime, garlic, ginger, sambal, hoisin sauce, soy sauce, peanut butter and honey, and stir well. In a large bowl, add half of your peanut sauce. Save the other half for dipping.

TO MAKE THE SKEWERS
Marinate your chicken in the large bowl with the peanut sauce for at least 10 minutes or overnight if you're making in advance. Meanwhile, soak your skewers in water if you are using wooden ones.

Line a baking sheet with aluminum foil and begin skewering the chicken. You want to pull the chicken as you skewer it, not push the pieces together, so that it lays thin and will cook evenly. Lay the skewers on the baking sheet.

Broil the skewers on high for 7 minutes until they're nicely charred and the chicken is cooked through. Serve warm, garnished with scallions and with extra dipping sauce on the side.

BABY NEEDS PIZZA HOME-BAKED REMEDY

SERVES 2

Annoyingly around the time of my pregnancy, my favorite brick-oven pizza restaurant stopped its delivery route eight blocks from our door. Despite giving fake addresses and trying to meet them halfway, my husband and I realized that to get our favorite pizza, just the way we like it, we were just going to have to make our own.

I use Mediterranean flat breads as my pizza crusts because they are easy to find and when prebaked, they achieve that toasty, crunchy taste of brick-oven pizza without needing a fancy oven or pizza stone.

This is our pizza how we like it. Feel free to do your toppings your way.

2 Mediterranean pita breads (frozen)

4 tbsp (59 ml) tomato sauce

6 slices fresh mozzarella cheese (4 oz [114 g])

18 slices pepperoni, divided (9 per pie)

10 jalapeño slices

8 fresh basil leaves

Red pepper flakes, to taste

Preheat your oven to 425°F (218°C).

Bake your pita breads for 3 minutes on the bottom oven rack, then flip them and bake for 3 minutes more until the flatbreads are crispy and toasty-brown on the top and bottom (if your flatbreads are not frozen, bake for 1 to 2 minutes per side).

Top each flatbread with 2 tablespoons (29 ml) of tomato sauce. Spread 3 slices of mozzarella on each flatbread, keeping it ¼ inch (0.5 cm) away from the edge. Then, top with the pepperoni, jalapeño and basil. Bake for 10 minutes. Then, if you want that bubbly, burned, brick-oven magic, broil on high for 2 to 3 minutes to finish, watching as you do and checking halfway. The broiling goes fast.

Cool for 1 to 2 minutes, then slice the flatbreads in quarters and serve warm with red pepper flakes.

FULL-TERM TWICE-BAKED POTATOES

SERVES 3

These potatoes are stuffed to the brim with goodness (much like you). They also let you enjoy the goat cheese you love but can't eat uncooked during pregnancy. Somewhat naughty and definitely nice on the stomach, these make a perfect light meal or side for dinner.

Whenever I bake potatoes I make extra so I can use leftovers in this recipe or for making home-style breakfast potatoes or steak fries. Here is the best way to bake them to achieve a perfectly crunchy, seasoned skin and a soft inside.

3 medium-large prebaked Idaho potatoes

2 tbsp (30 ml) olive oil

Sea salt and freshly cracked pepper

2 tbsp (30 ml) melted butter, divided

½ cup (119 ml) whole milk

4 oz (114 g) herbed goat cheese

TO BAKE YOUR POTATOES

Preheat your oven to 425°F (218°C).

Line a baking sheet with aluminum foil and prick your potatoes several times with the tines of a fork. Then, rub your potatoes with olive oil and season the skin with sea salt and freshly cracked pepper. Bake for 45 minutes to 1 hour until the skin is crispy and the insides tender when tested. I do this step in advance and refrigerate my potatoes once cooled.

TO MAKE THE TWICE-BAKED POTATOES

Preheat your oven to 350°F (177°C).

Line a baking sheet with aluminum foil for easy cleanup. Cut an oval circle on the top of each potato and remove. Scoop out the filling, leaving a ¼-inch (0.5-cm) shell. Place the filling into a large bowl and mix with 1 tablespoon (15 ml) of melted butter and all the milk. Mash to combine until smooth. Next, add the goat cheese and mix until thoroughly blended. Season with salt and pepper. Divide this delicious filling between the three potatoes and place the potatoes on the baking sheet. Bake for 25 minutes.

Remove your baking sheet from the oven and drizzle the tops of the potatoes with the remaining butter. Broil on high for 3 to 5 minutes (watching as you do to prevent burning) until the tops are a beautiful golden brown. Enjoy while warm.

NOTE: Although it may be tempting, don't add any additional fresh goat cheese after baking or nibble any as you cook. Goat cheese is a soft cheese and can contain listeria, so if you're pregnant, you don't want to eat it raw.

PREGO PICNIC CHILI LIME FRUIT CONES

SERVES 6

During pregnancy, you often need a fast snack that is both refreshing and tasty. In this recipe, the sweet fruit is heightened by just the right mix of sea salt, lime and chili powder. These cones are also a fun option for serving at a baby shower or warm weather picnic.

3 ripe yellow mangoes, peeled and sliced

2 English cucumbers, peeled, seeded and sliced

¼ seedless watermelon, chopped into sticks (I find it easiest to purchase the presliced wedge instead of an entire watermelon)

3 limes, quartered for seasoning

Chili powder to taste

Sea salt to taste

If you're making this just for yourself, the easiest way is to lay the mangoes, cucumbers and watermelon in a plastic container, drizzle them with lime and season them with chili powder and sea salt to your liking. Pack a fork, and you've got a light, refreshing meal on the go.

For party handouts, place the mangoes, cucumbers and watermelon into cups and place them on a tray. Leave the lime wedges, salt and chili powder on the side to allow guests to season to their liking.

TROPICAL TUMMY MANGO FAUX-'JITO

SERVES 1

During the first trimester, I, like many new moms, was trying to hide my pregnancy. This was a hard task for me since my social life revolved around eating and drinking. I decided the fancier I went with ordering fake drinks, the fewer questions I would be asked. A kindly bartender, some may call him a saint, created a mango "mojito" for me with spicy simple syrup that I've been craving since. This is so good you don't need to be pregnant to enjoy it.

This mocktail also rocks for mamas still fighting morning sickness. Mint and bubbles in seltzers have both been shown to help alleviate nausea.

JALAPEÑO SIMPLE SYRUP
½ cup (120 ml) water

½ cup (100 g) sugar

1 jalapeño sliced lengthwise, remove seeds if you don't want it to be too spicy or leave seeds if you love the heat

FAUX-'JITO
2 sprigs mint

1 lime, quartered

1½ oz (40 ml) jalapeño simple syrup (1 shot glass)

3 oz (89 ml) mango nectar

3 oz (89 ml) seltzer water

TO MAKE THE SIMPLE SYRUP
In a small saucepan, bring the water to a boil and stir in the sugar until dissolved. Remove from the heat and add the jalapeño. For a slight jalapeño flavor, remove after 15 minutes. Otherwise, leave it in until it reaches the intensity you like. Discard the jalapeño before serving.

TO MAKE THE FAUX-'JITO
In a large cocktail shaker, muddle your mint with the lime wedges and your simple syrup. Fill your shaker with ice and pour the mango nectar on top. Shake vigorously until the shaker feels very cool to the touch. Meanwhile, fill a rocks glass with ice. Pour your mango mojito into your glass and top with seltzer. Garnish with a lime wedge and extra mint.

STRAWBERRY "MARGARITA" FOR MAMAS

SERVES 2

It's hard to make a virgin margarita. So much of what makes a margarita fun is the kick of tequila, and I don't believe in just taking away the alcohol and calling something virgin. You can't omit a major ingredient and have the same flavors. So instead, I wanted to create a drink I would enjoy pregnant or not.

For starters, it had to be frozen. I also didn't want to add a ton of sugar so I opted for a fruit flavor. Then, finally, the coconut milk was the secret ingredient to make the drink feel, well, special. It added a creaminess and lusciousness that completed the "cocktail."

1 lime wedge

Kosher or cocktail salt

1½ cups (224 g) frozen strawberries

3 tbsp (45 ml) unsweetened coconut milk (full fat)

1 cup (247 ml) limeade (I like to use Simply Limeade)

Fresh strawberry for garnish

If you are rimming your glass with salt, do so beforehand. To rim the glass, rub a lime wedge around the edge of the glass. Fill a small plate with kosher or cocktail salt and dip your glass to lightly coat with salt.

In a good blender, puree the strawberries, coconut milk and limeade on high until smooth. Pour into your glass, and garnish with a slice of fresh strawberry. Sip while chilled.

BABY SHOWER "SANGRIA"

SERVES 1

Mocktails don't have to feel like you're drinking a juice box or sitting at the kids' table again. They can be just as spirited as the real thing and make you feel just as special, which is what a great cocktail does.

Sangria is a summer drink, but one of my favorite bars used to serve a version that was so wonderfully spicy with cinnamon and dark berries that it was perfect for winter as well. Here's a mocktail you can feel festive serving year-round.

The rooibos in the tea can be helpful for indigestion and infant colic.

COLD BREWED ICE TEA

10 decaf rooibos tea bags

7 cups (1.7 L) cold water

CINNAMON SIMPLE SYRUP

½ cup (120 ml) water

3 cinnamon sticks

½ cup (100 g) sugar

¼ cup (60 ml) sparkling water

Apple and orange slices for garnish

Frozen cranberries and a rosemary stick, if you want it to feel extra wintry

TO BREW THE TEA

In a large pitcher, add the tea bags and water. (This is for a strong tea. For a weaker tea use fewer tea bags.) Set the pitcher in the refrigerator and remove the tea bags after 1 hour or once the liquid is a rich orange-red color and the flavor is prominent when you try it.

TO MAKE THE SIMPLE SYRUP

In a small saucepan, bring the water with the cinnamon sticks to a boil. Then add the sugar and stir until dissolved. Leave the cinnamon sticks in as you allow the syrup to cool. Remove them before using.

TO MAKE THE "SANGRIA"

Mix ½ cup (120 ml) of tea and 2 teaspoons (10 ml) of simple syrup in an ice-filled glass and stir until mixed. Top with the sparkling water. Add the fruit, then finish with some frozen cranberries and a rosemary stick if desired.

FOODS TO AVOID WHEN EXPECTING

CHEESE

Avoid unpasteurized or soft cheeses such as brie and feta. Any grab-and-go salad that has feta, blue cheese, fresh mozzarella, brie or deli meat should be avoided. As long as the cheese is cooked (such as with the pizza and twice-baked potatoes recipes in this chapter) it is OK for consumption. Just make sure it is cooked through.

FRUITS AND VEGETABLES

Raw sprouts are not safe. They can contain salmonella, listeria or E. coli, and it is nearly impossible to wash them enough to get rid of the bacteria. Other vegetables and fruits can be washed under running water. The FDA does not recommend using soap, disinfectants or commercial-grade washes.

FISH AND SHELLFISH

Stay away from raw or smoked fish and raw oysters. Pregnant women can have two to three servings of most types of fish per week with the exception of king mackerel, marlin, orange roughy, shark, swordfish, tilefish and bigeye tuna. Those should be avoided due to potentially high levels of mercury. Fish such as Chilean sea bass, grouper, halibut, mahi-mahi, snapper, striped bass, albacore tuna (white tuna, canned, fresh and frozen) and yellowfin tuna should be limited to one serving per week or no more than 6 ounces (168 g). Fish caught for sport, as on a fishing trip, should also be avoided due to a lack of knowledge of potential contaminants. Mussels and clams and other fish and shellfish are safe as long as they are cooked properly.

MEAT

Raw or undercooked meats are also a no. Other culprits are lunch meats and hot dogs. These foods can contain a bacterium called *Listeria monocytogenes* that is associated with spontaneous abortion and stillbirth. To avoid listeriosis, make sure these processed meats are stored correctly and heated to steaming before eating.

EGGS

Eggs can be contaminated with salmonella. They won't hurt the fetus but may cause some diarrhea in Mom. So to be on the safe side, avoid runny eggs, Caesar dressing and hollandaise. Avoid homemade ice cream if the base hasn't been cooked.

FOODS TO LIMIT WHEN EXPECTING

NITRATES AND NITRITES

Nitrates and nitrites are a concern only if these foods are being consumed in excess. You will find nitrates in many cured meats (bacon and pepperoni) as well as in a lot of hot sauces.

CAFFEINE

Limit your caffeine intake from coffee, soft drinks and tea to under 200 mg a day. That's 12 ounces (360 ml) of coffee, 32 ounces (960 ml) of tea or five 12-ounce (360-ml) cans of soda (though that's a lot of soda; I'd recommend less).

FOOD SAFETY

Food safety in the kitchen is important at all times, but pregnancy may give you a heightened awareness of it. It is best to practice now so that once you begin introducing solids, you'll be a seasoned pro in the kitchen.

- Wash your hands thoroughly in warm, soapy water before and after cooking. This is especially important after handling raw meat, seafood and eggs but is also important when washing root vegetables and other ingredients. If you cook a lot with meat, it is nice if you can have a separate cutting board that is easily washed and sanitized.

- Wash all produce with water, and invest in a small vegetable scrub brush to scrub away residual dirt on root vegetables. Even if you are planning on peeling a fruit or vegetable, it is important to wash it first.

- Thoroughly wash any vegetables or herbs from the garden. Just because you grew it doesn't mean it can skip a good cleaning.

- Always date frozen food and don't allow items to thaw on the counter. Thaw any items in the refrigerator. It takes longer, but you can rest easy knowing you're not cultivating bacteria.

- Cook meat to its optimal cooking temperature. Cook seafood until the flesh is opaque (lobster), opaque and flaking (fish) or until shells open (mussels, clams and oysters). Chicken, ground meat and turkey should be cooked to 165°F (74°C). The temperature for beef depends on how you are cooking it. If you're pregnant, steak should be cooked to 170°F (77°C). So pregnancy may not be the best time to visit a great steakhouse unless you enjoy your meat well done.

- When dining outside, cover any sitting food so it won't attract bugs.

- Have a separate cleaning system for your pump, baby bottles and, later, baby's food. Since dishes that have touched raw meat or egg may end up in your sink, and you don't want food items on bottles or pumps anyway, this is important. I find it easiest to have a separate cleaning space and drying space for these items. It doesn't take much space; I have room even in my small NYC kitchen.

GESTATIONAL DIABETES

Gestational diabetes mellitus (GDM) is a type of diabetes first diagnosed during pregnancy and is most closely related to type 2 diabetes. Usually gestational diabetes goes away within 6 months of delivery, however, nearly 50 percent of women diagnosed with GDM will have it in a subsequent pregnancy. Uncontrolled GDM can lead to an increased risk of spontaneous abortion, stillbirth, birth defects and neonatal death. If you are diagnosed with GDM, consultating a registered dietitian for dietary management is key.

GESTATIONAL DIABETES GENERAL DIETARY PLAN

* Eat whole grains, vegetables and fruits

* Eat minimally processed, nutrient-dense foods (nuts, meats, dairy, fruits, veggies and quinoa)

* Eat appropriate portion sizes, especially of foods containing carbohydrates

* Limit intake of simple sugars in foods and beverages (cakes, donuts, cookies, sodas, sweet teas, fruit juices, fruit punches and blends, lemonades and Gatorade)

* Limit glycemic index foods (white rice, potatoes, white bread, juices and sugar-sweetened beverages)

* Eat three meals and at least one snack daily

To better control blood glucose and slow the absorption of carbohydrates, eat carbohydrates with a protein or a fat. Many people are under the impression that they need to cut out carbohydrates if they have any type of diabetes. This can be dangerous, especially for a pregnant woman. The fetus needs a minimum of 175 grams of carbohydrates daily to meet the fetal brain's needs.

GETTING READY FOR BABY

Getting ready for a baby is a lot like getting ready for a 1950s nuclear attack: You want to be sure that your family can survive on only what's in the house while you hunker down. I'll leave it to you to stock up on toiletries, but what you also need to stock up on are home-cooked meals. After your baby is born, you'll want to return to normalcy. Eating the foods you enjoy as a family and not feeling like you have to order takeout or rely on the kindness of visiting friends or family for sustenance gives you that normalcy you'll crave. This chapter gives you some great freezer meals and pantry staples to get you through the first crucial weeks after you bring your baby home. I also include some recipes for those last weeks when you finally feel ready—then more than ready—for your baby's arrival.

HOME-BAKED GRANOLA

MAKES ABOUT 7 CUPS (563 G)

Having a large batch of homemade granola helps you prepare for countless breakfasts and snacks. This recipe is very simple, packed with fiber and has the perfect crunch.

5 cups (400 g) old-fashioned rolled oats

½ cup (64 g) unsalted sunflower seeds (or pecan halves)

1 cup (92 g) sliced almonds

½ cup (120 ml) olive oil

¼ cup (59 ml) honey

¼ cup (59 ml) 100% maple syrup

½ tsp salt

Preheat your oven to 325°F (163°C).

In a large bowl, mix the oats, sunflower seeds and almonds together.

In a small bowl, mix the olive oil, honey, maple syrup and salt. Pour your honey mixture over your oats and stir very well until every oat is coated.

Divide the oat mixture between two large baking sheets, spreading the oats into one layer on each sheet to ensure even baking. Bake both sheets on two center racks for 10 minutes. Toss the granola with a wooden spatula to prevent sticking. Bake 10 to 12 minutes more until golden brown. Toss once more to prevent sticking.

Turn off your oven and leave the granola to cool completely. Do not store until completely cool or you will lose that glorious crunch.

MAKE AHEAD, ENJOY LATER PANCAKE MIX

MAKES 1 BATCH OF PANCAKES

Making pancake mix ahead of time is basically a way to save yourself the trouble of making pancakes from scratch while you are sleep deprived and struggling through your morning. I usually make three batches at once so that I have three awesome breakfasts all stocked up in the pantry. That way when I want pancakes, all I need to do is add milk, eggs and butter.

2 cups (250 g) all-purpose flour

½ tsp baking soda

2 tsp (8 g) baking powder

½ tsp salt

1 tbsp (13 g) sugar

In a large bowl, whisk the flour, baking soda, baking powder, salt and sugar together. Store in a plastic resealable bag, Mason jar or plastic container and write the date on it. This mix lasts for 3 months in an air-safe container.

NOTE: Mark the date you open your baking soda and baking powder on the jar. It affects your recipes tremendously. For best use, discard 6 months after opening.

BLUEBERRY BUTTERMILK PANCAKES

MAKES 14 TO 18 PANCAKES

When you're ready to use your pancake mix, follow these easy steps for the fluffiest, most heavenly pancakes.

---

1 batch Make Ahead, Enjoy Later Pancake Mix (page 47)

2 cups (473 ml) buttermilk

2 eggs

4 tbsp (59 ml) melted butter, plus more for cooking

1 cup (148 g) blueberries

100% maple syrup for serving

Place your pancake mix in a large bowl. In a medium bowl, combine your buttermilk and eggs and whip until smooth. Add the melted butter and stir to combine.

Slowly pour your wet ingredients into your dry and mix until just combined. Don't overwork your batter. I like to fold it in with a spatula until I no longer see clumps of flour. Once combined, add the blueberries.

Heat your griddle, cast-iron or sauté pan over medium heat. Add a pat of butter and ladle a small circle of pancake mix into the pan. Cook the pancakes for 2 to 3 minutes per side. Flip when you see the outer edge of your pancake begin to solidify and small bubbles form in the center. Keep checking your heat between batches to make sure the pancakes aren't cooking beyond a nice golden brown. I also like to keep the oven on 200°F (93°C) and pop in a baking sheet of finished pancakes, so when I'm done cooking all the pancakes, the first ones are still warm. Serve warm with maple syrup.

NOTE: Most people don't keep a steady stock of buttermilk in their refrigerator. If you find yourself with leftover buttermilk and don't know how to use it, make a creamy dressing or use it to marinate chicken before frying. Or mix it into a batch of my 3 Cheese Chile Cornbread (page 184). It is a secret ingredient that you'll find yourself using time and again.

FREEZE-BY-THE-BATCH TOMATO SAUCE

MAKES 7 CUPS (2 L)

You may ask why bother to make tomato sauce when there are so many store-bought options, but try this and you'll understand. This tomato sauce is the perfect base for so many recipes, easy to cook and delicious when served simply over good pasta and topped with freshly grated mozzarella cheese.

This scrumptious sauce is also loaded with healthy fats! Fats are important during pregnancy because they are used as energy for fetal growth and can provide fat-soluble vitamins. So be sure to enjoy a spoonful or two fresh from the pot before you store it away for later meals.

¼ cup (60 ml) extra virgin olive oil

½ cup (76 g) finely chopped yellow onion

3 cloves garlic, finely sliced

2 (28-oz [794-g]) cans whole plum tomatoes

¾ tsp salt

1 tsp sugar, optional (it does help to bring out the sweetness of the tomatoes)

¼ cup (6 g) fresh basil leaves

In a large stockpot, add the olive oil and onions. Cook on medium-high heat for 3 minutes and then add the garlic and cook for 1 minute, allowing the onions to soften and the flavor to infuse the oil. Add the tomatoes, salt, sugar and basil, and stir to combine. Cook for 15 minutes on medium-high heat, allowing the tomatoes to soften and become sweet and jammy. Blend with an immersion blender until the sauce is the consistency you like.

DINNER-IN-A-PINCH CLASSIC PESTO

MAKES 2 CUPS (473 ML)

Having pesto stored away is always a good idea. This pesto can be used as a sauce for pasta, a spread for sandwiches or a topping for eggs. It takes very little space in your freezer but gives you so many opportunities for great meals when you don't have the time to cook.

1½ cups (36 g) packed basil leaves

¾ cup (135 g) grated Parmesan cheese

¼ cup (34 g) pine nuts (or equal parts walnuts as a substitution)

¾ cup (180 ml) extra virgin olive oil

Salt to taste

Puree the ingredients in a strong blender or food processor until smooth. Freeze for later use or enjoy immediately.

If you are trying to save freezer space, you can even freeze in a strong, resealable plastic bag, laying it flat so that the pesto freezes in one small sheet.

NOTE: As a variation, replace the pine nuts with walnuts. Walnuts have omega-3 fatty acids, which are essential for fetal brain and eye development. This can help a lot of pregnant moms who are limited in their fish intake due to mercury restrictions during pregnancy.

FREEZER-FRIENDLY CHICKEN CHILE ENCHILADAS

MAKES 10 ENCHILADAS

My mom made me this recipe on her visit after I gave birth. It was such a gratifying meal: chicken, rice and just enough spice. We loved it so much that on subsequent visits she would always leave an extra batch in the freezer, the way only a mom can.

The bonus during your pregnancy is that the cilantro in this recipe is a good source of folate. Adequate intake of folate during pregnancy protects against some types of neurological birth defects. Isn't it wonderful when something you already love has added health benefits?

SIMPLE ENCHILADA SAUCE

2 cups (473 ml) green salsa

½ cup (118 ml) chicken stock

ENCHILADAS

2 cups (322 g) cooked jasmine rice

2 cups (280 g) cooked and finely diced chicken

1 tsp cumin

1 (4-oz [141-g]) can diced green chiles

1 cup (50 g) diced scallions (4 scallions)

1 cup (16 g) cilantro leaves, chopped

3 cups (362 g) grated cheddar cheese, divided

10 medium-size flour tortillas (6 inches [15 cm] in diameter each)

Sour cream, avocado, cilantro and jalapeño for garnish, optional

Preheat your oven to 375°F (190°C).

TO MAKE THE SAUCE

In a medium bowl, mix the green salsa and chicken stock, and set it aside.

TO MAKE THE ENCHILADAS

In a large bowl, mix the rice, chicken, cumin, chiles, scallions, cilantro and 1 cup (121 g) of the grated cheddar. Top with ¾ cup (205 g) of enchilada sauce and mix well.

Add ½ cup (118 ml) of enchilada sauce each to two 9 × 9-inch (23 × 23-cm) baking dishes and spread evenly. Top each tortilla with ½ cup (80 g) of the rice-and-chicken mixture and roll to finish. Lay the rolled tortillas in a tight row with the seam down in your first baking dish. Repeat until all the tortillas are rolled.

Divide the remaining enchilada sauce between the two baking dishes, making sure to spread it over the top and sides of every enchilada. Top each baking dish with 1 cup (121 g) of grated cheese, spreading it evenly. Freeze one pan of enchiladas for later and bake the other for dinner.

Bake for 30 minutes and cool for 10 minutes. Garnish to taste with sour cream, avocado, cilantro and jalapeño.

MOM-TO-BE SAUSAGE AND VEGGIE ZITI

SERVES 6 TO 8

This recipe makes two dinner portions, one for immediate enjoyment and another as the perfect freezer meal. Scrumptiously cheesy and absolutely comforting, you'll really appreciate having a meal in the bank once baby arrives.

Also, later down the line for toddlers, this recipe is loaded with hidden veggies. Vegetable intake recommendations for kids range from one to three cups per day, but most children eat less than one-half cup per day. Use this delicious recipe to sneak in those extra servings.

2 tbsp (30 ml) olive oil, divided

12 oz (340 g) chicken sausage (precooked), sliced into ¼-inch (0.5-cm) rounds

1½ cups (186 g) diced zucchini (1 medium zucchini)

1 cup (156 g) frozen spinach (or 2 cups [60 g] fresh)

1 lb (454 g) fusilli pasta

26 oz (728 ml) tomato sauce

½ cup (90 g) grated Parmesan cheese

1 cup (60 g) chopped fresh basil

16 oz (454 g) freshly grated mozzarella cheese, divided

Preheat your oven to 425°F (218°C).

In a large sauté pan, add 1 tablespoon (15 ml) of olive oil and cook the chicken sausage on medium-high heat for 3 minutes per side until golden brown. Once browned, remove to a separate plate.

In the same pan, add the remaining oil and cook the zucchini for 2 minutes per side until softened and caramelized. Then add the spinach and cook until warmed (2 to 3 minutes for frozen, 1 to 2 minutes for fresh).

Meanwhile, cook the pasta according to package directions. I add 1 to 2 minutes when I'm sharing with my toddler because softer noodles are his favorite.

Once the pasta is cooked, drain in a colander. In the pasta pot, mix the sausage, vegetable mixture and tomato sauce. Add the noodles, then stir in the Parmesan, basil and half of the mozzarella. Spoon this delicious mixture into two 8 × 8-inch (20.5 × 20.5-cm) baking dishes and top with the remaining mozzarella. Cover one dish with aluminum foil and freeze. Bake the other dish in the oven for 20 minutes or until the cheese is melted and the tomato sauce begins to bubble.

BLACK BEAN AND QUINOA BURGERS

MAKES 6 BURGERS

I have always loved veggie burgers even though I'm an avid omnivore. These are so flavorful you won't miss the meat, and they make for a great family dinner. It is also nice to have patties premade so you have a lunch ready to go in a hurry. This recipe is very toddler friendly and easy to cut into fun shapes for children who have moved on to finger foods.

1 tbsp (15 ml) olive oil

½ cup (90 g) finely diced red pepper

½ cup (76 g) finely diced red onion

½ cup (82 g) frozen sweet corn

2 tbsp (2 g) minced cilantro leaves

2 cloves garlic, minced

½ tsp onion powder

½ tsp garlic powder

½ tsp sea salt

½ tsp smoked paprika

1 tsp cumin

1 cup (185 g) cooked red quinoa

1 (14.5-oz [411-g]) can black beans, rinsed and drained

1 large egg

½ cup (54 g) dry bread crumbs

¼ cup (31 g) all-purpose flour

TOPPINGS

Sharp cheddar cheese

Avocado

Lettuce

Tomato

Red onion

In a medium sauté pan, add the olive oil, red pepper, onion and corn, and sauté for 3 to 4 minutes on medium-high heat until just beginning to soften. Add the cilantro and garlic, and cook for another 2 minutes, then remove from the heat. Mix in the onion powder, garlic powder, salt, paprika, cumin and quinoa until they're thoroughly incorporated.

In a medium bowl with a good fork, mash the black beans until about three-quarters of them are mashed, but you still see some whole beans. Add the sautéed vegetable-and-quinoa mixture from the pan to the beans, and mix to combine. Add the egg, bread crumbs and flour, and mix thoroughly.

To form into patties, lay a sheet of wax paper on top of a baking sheet, and make sure you have enough space for this baking sheet in your freezer. Wet your hands to make it easier to form the patties. Divide the bean-and-quinoa mixture into 6 equal parts and press them into patties. Lay the finished patties on the baking sheet and freeze for at least 1 hour to overnight. Freezing makes the burgers hold together much better when cooking.

To heat the burgers, remove them from the freezer and grill or panfry until they're darkened on top and cooked through to the middle. These work great on an indoor grill and also cooked in a sauté pan.

To cook in a pan, add 1 tablespoon (15 ml) of oil to the pan and cook on medium heat for 4 to 5 minutes per side until the outsides are browned and the insides are cooked through. Then add cheese, cover the pan and let it melt for a minute before serving.

My favorite toppings are sharp cheddar cheese, avocado, lettuce, tomato and red onion.

FORK-FREE TURKEY AND MUSHROOM HAND PIES

MAKES 20 HAND PIES

These are beyond ridiculously tasty! They are also very easy to eat while holding a baby, walking around the house and reaching for something (basically every mom's life). I got the base recipe for these from my good friend Michelle, who is the empress of empanadas and also a pediatric nurse in the ER . . . basically, she is a saint.

2 (10-count) packages discos (found in the freezer section at a grocery store)

1 tbsp (15 ml) extra virgin olive oil

½ cup (76 g) finely diced white onion

8 oz (227 g) white mushrooms, cleaned, stems removed and diced

2 cloves garlic, minced

1 lb (454 g) ground turkey

1 tsp cumin

¼ cup (59 ml) green salsa

2 tbsp (29 ml) hot sauce, optional

¼ cup (4 g) chopped fresh cilantro

Sea salt

8 oz (224 g) shredded mozzarella cheese

1 egg, for egg wash

1 tbsp (15 ml) water

FOR SERVING
Hot sauce

Salsa fresca

Defrost the discos; they take about 2 hours. That seems like a lot of time, but it is mindless time, so just do it at the start of the day and come back to it later. I find it much easier than making dough from scratch and having to clean up.

Preheat your oven to 400°F (204°C).

In a large sauté pan, add the olive oil and sauté the onion for 2 minutes on medium-high heat. Add the mushrooms and garlic and cook for another 2 minutes until the mushrooms have softened and started to release some moisture. Add the turkey, cumin, green salsa, hot sauce, if desired, and cilantro, and cook for 4 to 6 minutes until the turkey is fully cooked. Season with salt.

To assemble, line two baking sheets with parchment paper and lay out as many discos as you can fit. Then take about 2 tablespoons (25 g) of your turkey filling and place it in the center of each disco. You may have a little extra filling at the end. Top with a large pinch of mozzarella cheese. Fold your filled disco in half and press along the open edges with a fork to seal. You want to make sure to seal it well so that your hand pies don't open and release their filling during baking. I often pinch the seam with my fingers before finishing with a fork to seal.

In a small bowl, whisk your egg with the water to make an egg wash. Brush your finished hand pies all along the top and seam with the egg wash. Bake for 25 to 28 minutes until golden brown. Eat once cool or freeze to enjoy later.

TO FREEZE
Allow to cool and then plop your baking sheets in the freezer. Freeze on the sheet for at least an hour before storing in a gallon-size plastic bag.

TO REHEAT
Microwave frozen hand pies for 1 to 2 minutes, or reheat in the oven at 350°F (177°C) for about 10 minutes or in the toaster oven on low until warmed through. Serve with hot sauce or salsa fresca.

40-WEEKS-AND-COUNTING SPICY EGGPLANT PARMESAN

SERVES 4

OK, some old wives' tales may be tastier than they are true, but I've always heard that a good Eggplant Parmesan can help induce labor. I didn't try it myself because my son surprised me by being a week early. But I guarantee that if all my relatives had flown out, and we were all twiddling our thumbs waiting for him to be born, I would have eaten anything that anyone told me to in order to speed his little journey into the world.

Eggplant is also rich in fiber and a good carbohydrate substitute in heavy Italian food. Use eggplant as a healthy substitute for breaded meats and pasta to make for gestational diabetes–friendly meals!

Extra virgin olive oil

1 large eggplant

2 eggs

2 tbsp (30 ml) water

1 (8-oz [227-g]) can dry bread crumbs

Sea salt and freshly cracked pepper

3 cups (709 ml) tomato sauce, divided

8 oz (227 g) mozzarella cheese, sliced

4 tbsp (45 g) grated Parmesan cheese

1 tbsp (5 g) red pepper flakes, adjust to taste

¼ cup (6 g) fresh basil leaves

Preheat your oven to 400°F (204°C).

Line 2 baking sheets with aluminum foil and drizzle olive oil on each. Rub your oil around to coat the sheets evenly.

Peel your eggplant then slice it into ¼-inch (0.5-cm) rounds. In a medium bowl with enough space for dipping your eggplant slices, whip your eggs with the water to form your egg wash. In another bowl, add your bread crumbs. Dip your eggplant slices in your egg wash, allowing any excess to drip off, and then dip them into your bread crumbs. Place the coated eggplant slices on your prepared baking sheets.

Bake in the oven for 12 minutes or until golden brown on the bottom. Drizzle the eggplant tops generously with oil before flipping and baking for 12 minutes on the other side. The finished slices should be golden brown on both sides. Season the finished eggplant with salt and pepper.

Spray a 15 × 10-inch (38 × 25.5-cm) baking dish with cooking spray, then add 1 cup (263 ml) of tomato sauce. You want to cook this meal in one layer. If you don't have a baking dish large enough, use two smaller ones. Lay out the eggplant slices in one layer with slices slightly overlapping. Cover with another 2 cups (473 ml) of tomato sauce, making sure to coat all slices, and then top with mozzarella. Next, sprinkle with Parmesan, red pepper flakes and fresh basil. Bake for 15 to 20 minutes until the cheese is melted. Cool, then serve warm.

BABY'S EVICTION NOTICE PINEAPPLE TERIYAKI CHICKEN STIR-FRY

SERVES 6

I love a good stir-fry for dinner. Since pineapple is said to speed delivery, this recipe serves two purposes: It's a tasty and easy meal and it gets your little bundle of joy into the world a little faster—or here's to hoping! The cashews in this recipe are a good source of zinc, which aids healing, making this the perfect prebaby meal!

1 cup (137 g) roasted cashew halves

3 tbsp (45 ml) vegetable oil, divided

2 lbs (907 g) chicken breast, sliced into bite-size strips

1 white onion, thinly sliced

2 bell peppers, diced

2 cups (330 g) diced pineapple

1 bunch scallions, cut into 1-inch (2.5-cm) long strips, stems removed

¾ cup (177 ml) teriyaki sauce

½ tsp cornstarch

1 tbsp (15 ml) soy sauce

Jasmine rice for serving

Heat a large frying pan on medium-high heat. Add the cashews, and toast until just golden, about 2 to 3 minutes, tossing once or twice. Watch the cashews so they don't burn. Set them aside on a plate once toasted.

Add 2 tablespoons (30 ml) of the vegetable oil, and sear the chicken strips for 2 to 3 minutes before flipping to sear the other side. You don't want to stir the chicken as it is cooking because you want it to pick up that nice golden-brown color. Once seared on both sides, immediately remove from the pan to another plate.

Add 1 tablespoon (15 ml) of oil and your sliced onion to the pan. Sauté for 4 to 5 minutes on medium-high heat, stirring once, until softened and just caramelized. Remove from the pan and add the bell peppers. Add additional oil as needed. Sauté for 4 to 5 minutes, turning once, until browned and softened. Remove from the pan. Add the pineapple to the pan and cook for 4 minutes until caramelized and golden. Toss in the scallions in the final minute of cooking. Remove all ingredients to a plate before cooking the sauce.

Add teriyaki sauce to the pan and bring to a boil. In a small bowl, mix your cornstarch with soy sauce and stir until a watery paste forms. Whisk your paste into your teriyaki mixture until it thickens, then return all the ingredients to the pan and toss until coated. Serve on a bed of jasmine rice.

TIPS AND MYTHS ON SPEEDING DELIVERY AFTER 40 WEEKS

If you google "What can I eat to induce labor?" you will find many different answers from basil and oregano teas to castor oil to spicy foods. However, to date, there is no conclusive research that any of these inducers actually work. I included two recipes in this book said to induce labor because, as with the Chinese calendar, which some parents swear predicts gender, many moms and dads out there will answer under oath that a certain meal helped them speed their little one's journey into the world.

Just remember, although you may be uncomfortable and ready to get that baby out, there are several benefits to waiting. More time in the womb allows the baby to build muscle and strength, reduces risk of infection and jaundice and may increase brain development. Plus, you can always take that time to get a pedicure predelivery, enjoy one last date night with your partner or try to sleep in, because in a few days you'll be missing your bed very much.

DATES FOR YOUR THIRD TRIMESTER

- Binge-watch your favorite shows in bed. This is a wonderful indulgence, and you'll miss these days when your viewing time caters more to children's programming than to the latest dramatic series.

- Take a sleep-in date on the weekend and challenge your partner to see who can doze longer. Sleep is so underrated. Take advantage while you still can.

- Go to all your favorite restaurants, the smaller the tables and fancier the food the better. It won't be long until you'll be choosing restaurants for their stroller parking and changing tables in the bathroom.

- See every movie in the theater that you can, especially Oscar nominees. A movie date is a costly luxury once you start footing babysitting bills.

- Wear a stupidly low-cut dress to show off your cleavage. For now, that impressive rack is just for show. (Bonus if you wear something that is silk or dry-clean only because those clothing items will quickly be relocated to the far recesses of your closet.)

- Take ridiculously long showers with the door locked.

- Go shopping and buy something for each other that's not baby related.

- Go to concerts, art museums, theaters and all other cultural venues that you can get to. It takes a long time for a baby to catch up to your cultural agenda—though museums, those of the "please touch" variety, especially, can be amazing fun once your baby hits the toddler years.

BUILDING YOUR PANTRY

Here's a list of the pantry items you'll be using to make the delicious recipes throughout this book. A well-stocked pantry leaves you options. The added benefit is many meals can be made almost exclusively from pantry items, sparing you a last-minute trip to the grocery store when you're already exhausted.

BAKING
- All-purpose flour
- Baking powder
- Baking soda
- Brown sugar
- Canned pumpkin (100% pure pumpkin)
- Cornmeal
- Cornstarch
- Honey (not for children under one year)
- Maple syrup
- Nuts: almonds, cashews, pecans, pine nuts, sunflower seeds and walnuts
- Sugar
- Vanilla extract
- Whole wheat flour

FROZEN FOODS
- Carrots
- Berries
- Broccoli
- Mediterranean flatbreads (I store them in the freezer to keep handy)
- Peas
- Spinach
- Sweet corn

GRAINS AND PASTA
- Arborio rice (for risotto)
- Bread crumbs (panko are best and the easiest option for avoiding added corn syrup)
- Jasmine rice
- Oats (old-fashioned rolled oats, not instant)
- Pasta: ditalini, egg noodles, fusilli, linguine, penne, orzo, rotini and star pasta
- Quinoa
- Ramen noodles
- Soba noodles

HOT SAUCES
- Sambal
- Sriracha
- Tapatío

OILS
- Canola or vegetable oil
- Extra virgin olive oil
- Sesame oil

SAUCES
- Chicken stock
- Coconut milk (full fat)
- Green salsa
- Hoisin
- Liquid smoke
- Low-sodium soy sauce
- Tahini
- Thai green curry paste
- Vegetable stock
- Worcestershire sauce

SPICES
- Black pepper (a pepper mill is best, so you can enjoy it freshly cracked)
- Cayenne
- Cinnamon
- Chili powder
- Cumin
- Dry mustard
- Garlic powder
- Ginger
- Nutmeg
- Onion powder
- Oregano
- Parsley
- Red pepper flakes
- Sea salt
- Sesame seeds
- Smoked paprika
- Thyme
- Turmeric

OTHER
- Canned beans: black, pink, red kidney, navy, white
- Canned chipotle peppers in adobo sauce
- Canned diced tomatoes
- Canned green chiles
- Dijon mustard
- Peanut butter
- Mayonnaise
- Sweet chili sauce

BREASTFEEDING FOODS

I remember preparing for my son's night-feeding sessions with OCD precision. I'd have a hair tie around my wrist, a cardigan draped over the doorknob and the ever-crucial glass(es) of water in every corner of my apartment where I nursed. Each night, I would check my setup, then I would pray as I lay down that I would get at least four hours of uninterrupted sleep.

Breastfeeding takes a lot of energy. Mom needs to eat, and food has to be readily handy because it will often be eaten while holding, and sometimes even feeding, a child. These recipes aim for complete meals and easy snacks that can be made in batches and grabbed as the need strikes.

GODDESS DRESSING WITH CRUDITÉS

SERVES 8 TO 10 (MAKES ABOUT 1½ CUPS [355 ML])

I have always been a fan of any dressing with *goddess* on the label. It doesn't matter the brand; it's normally good. My husband isn't ashamed to tap into his inner goddess either. Something about the fresh herbs and creaminess makes greens feel a little more spectacular. This is a wonderful dip for a breastfeeding mom who needs a reminder that she is important and powerful.

Did you know that your milk carries the flavors of compounds in foods like mint, garlic and vanilla? So you're already introducing new flavors to your baby even before you've introduced solids!

GODDESS DIP

½ cup (118 ml) Greek yogurt

½ cup (118 ml) sour cream

1 tbsp (15 ml) lemon juice

2 cloves garlic

1 cup (24 g) fresh basil leaves

¼ cup (13 g) chives

Sea salt and freshly cracked pepper to taste

CRUDITÉS

4 radishes, cleaned and quartered

3 Persian cucumbers, quartered

½ cup (32 g) sugar snap peas

½ cup (90 g) sliced yellow bell pepper

½ cup (90 g) sliced orange bell pepper

1 cup (149 g) cherry tomatoes

4 small carrots, peeled and halved or quartered (depending on size)

TO MAKE THE GODDESS DIP

In a food processor or strong blender, combine the yogurt, sour cream, lemon juice, garlic, basil and chives, and puree on high until smooth. Season to taste with salt and pepper. Let it rest in the refrigerator for at least 30 minutes so that the dip has a chance to set and thicken.

Serve with the crudités for dipping.

CALCIUM-RICH WHIPPED FETA DIP

MAKES 1¾ CUPS (414 ML)

This feta dip is so extremely tasty, I used to order takeout from my favorite Greek restaurant for it alone. My deep love and growing consumption of this dip made it imperative that I master the recipe myself. The resulting dip is delicious eaten with freshly toasted pita and also makes for a killer sandwich spread. For the breastfeeding mom, it is packed with calcium!

1 to 2 small fresh jalapeños (if you don't like spice, use less or substitute with ¼ of a poblano pepper)

8 oz (227 g) Greek feta (full fat and creamy)

¼ cup (59 ml) Greek yogurt (full fat)

½ cup (120 g) whipped cream cheese (full fat)

1 tbsp (15 ml) olive oil

2 tbsp (30 ml) vegetable oil

Toasted pita bread for dipping

Begin by holding your jalapeños with tongs over a gas burner. Cook them for about 5 minutes, until the skins are blackened and charred. Remove the skin with the back of a paring knife, and then slice the peppers and discard the seeds, charred skin and stems.

In a food processor, combine the jalapeños, feta, yogurt, cream cheese, olive oil and vegetable oil, and pulse until creamy and smooth.

I like to warm the dip ever so slightly either in the microwave for 30 seconds or briefly in the oven in an ovenproof dish before serving. Heating the dip makes it easier to spread. Serve with warm toasted pita.

MAMA'S GUACAMOLE

SERVES 4

The best ingredients make the best guacamole. Don't even bother making this recipe if you can't find two perfectly ripe avocados because it will just be disappointing. Also, don't judge an avocado by its exterior color; go by feel. A perfect avocado should give just slightly when pressed with your fingertips. It should slice like butter and the inside should be a soft pale yellow–green color.

This recipe is also great for getting healthy fats into your diet. In each feeding, your baby will get two types of breast milk: foremilk and hind milk. Fore milk is higher in carbohydrates, and hind milk is higher in fat. In fact, 60 to 80 percent of the calories in hind milk come from fat. The benefit? The fat in the hind milk keeps a baby fuller longer, which may mean a longer night's sleep for you.
I can't think of a better reason to eat guacamole!

2 ripe Hass avocados

1 lime, juiced

2 tbsp (29 ml) green salsa

2 tbsp (11 g) minced jalapeño
(1 small jalapeño seeded and
deveined), optional

¼ cup (4 g) cilantro leaves, chopped

½ cup (90 g) finely diced ripe
tomatoes (tomatoes on a vine are
my favorite)

2 tbsp (25 g) finely minced
red onion

Sea salt

In a small bowl, mash the avocados until smooth. Add the lime juice and green salsa. Mix again until smooth. Next, stir in the jalapeño, cilantro, tomatoes and red onion. Season to taste with salt. Serve immediately.

If refrigerating before use, cover the bowl with plastic wrap and press down into the top of the guacamole to remove any air. This will keep the guacamole from browning before serving.

HOME-STYLE SALSA

MAKES 3 CUPS (709 ML)

Fresh salsa is the best because it is a conduit for eating more tortilla chips. It has been argued by some who know me that if I were what I ate, I would be a tortilla chip, or, more accurately, one large nacho. My toddler son, my true flesh and blood, understands how good these chips are. He slowly feeds them to me whenever he sees me eating them, serving me first before he takes a little nibble. If he could only learn to dip better, we would be unstoppable!

---

4 plum tomatoes (405 g), tops removed and quartered

3 medium tomatillos (198 g), husks and stems removed and quartered

1 small red onion (151 g), quartered

1½ limes, juiced

1 tbsp (15 ml) adobo sauce (from a can of chipotle peppers in adobo)

2 chipotle peppers (from the same can of chipotle peppers in adobo), optional

1 small jalapeño, seeded, deveined and quartered, optional

1 cup (16 g) cilantro leaves

½ tsp salt

1 tbsp (15 ml) olive oil

Add all the ingredients to a strong blender or food processor. Pulse until the ingredients are mixed well and no large chunks remain. Be sure to use a spatula to wipe the sides of the blender to catch all the ingredients before your final pulse.

As this salsa sits, the tomato juice makes it a bit watery. For easiest dipping, drain the salsa using a slotted spoon before serving.

GOTTA REHYDRATE CUCUMBER TOMATO SALAD

SERVES 4

Did you know that 20 percent of our water intake comes from food? Want to boost that? Try this recipe. Cucumbers are 96 percent water and tomatoes are 94 percent water. For a nursing mother, hydration is key! This salad is so simple that you can make it in a couple of minutes.

2½ cups (375 g) diced hothouse cucumber (1 to 2 cucumbers depending on size)

1 cup (152 g) finely diced red onion

2 cups (360 g) diced plum or grape tomato (4 plum tomatoes or 10 oz [284 g] grape tomatoes)

1 tbsp (15 ml) freshly squeezed lemon juice (1 lemon)

3 tbsp (45 ml) olive oil

1 cup (60 g) parsley leaves, finely chopped

Sea salt and freshly cracked pepper

In a medium bowl, combine the cucumber, onion, tomatoes, lemon juice, oil and parsley, and season to taste with salt and pepper. Don't be stingy on the seasonings because they help bring out the flavor. Refrigerate and serve chilled.

NOTE: If you want to bring the recipe up a notch, you can also add in a diced Hass avocado or crumbled feta.

ORZO AND SUNDRIED TOMATO SALAD

SERVES 4

This is a salad and pasta dish all in one. It is filling, fresh and incredibly easy to make in advance, so you can grab it whenever you need to.

1 cup (100 g) orzo

¼ cup (38 g) crumbled feta

½ cup (27 g) sundried tomatoes, sliced in thin strips

2 tbsp (30 ml) olive oil

1 tsp fresh lemon juice

¼ cup (38 g) finely chopped red onion

2 tbsp (8 g) chopped fresh parsley

1 cup (20 g) arugula

Sea salt and freshly cracked pepper

Boil the orzo for 8 to 9 minutes, stirring frequently, and then drain in a colander with fine holes so the orzo doesn't escape. In a large bowl, mix the orzo with the feta, sundried tomatoes, oil, lemon juice, onion, parsley and arugula. Season to taste with salt and pepper.

I like mine slightly warmed so the cooked pasta melts a bit of the feta. This dish is also delicious chilled.

GRAB-AND-GO GREEN PASTA SALAD

SERVES 8 TO 10

This pasta salad tastes just as good hot or cold. Its versatility makes it an ideal grab-and-go option for the mom at the mercy of a small child.

4 cups (284 g) frozen broccoli florets

6 oz (170 g) green beans, stems removed and sliced in half

1 cup (145 g) frozen sweet peas

1 lb (454 g) rotini pasta, cooked according to package instructions

1 cup (252 g) Dinner-in-a-Pinch Classic Pesto (page 52)

In a large pot, bring 1 inch (2.5 cm) of water to a boil (you don't want the water to reach above the bottom of your steamer basket).

Add your broccoli and steam, covered in the basket, for about 2 minutes until tender. Remove to a colander and shock with cold water if you want to preserve the color. Add the green beans to the steamer basket and cook for about 2 minutes until tender but still crunchy. Remove to the colander and shock with cold water. Steam the peas until they're no longer frozen, about 2 minutes. Remove to the colander and shock with cold water.

Mix the pasta and pesto, then add the steamed vegetables. Stir to combine. Enjoy immediately or refrigerate for later.

QUICK-FIX TOFU AND KALE STIR-FRY

SERVES 4 TO 6

This recipe is easy to put together and pretty darn delicious. Tofu is an excellent source of protein and contains all essential amino acids, making this a great meat alternative for vegans and vegetarians and an option for Meatless Mondays!

3 tbsp (45 ml) sesame oil, divided

1 package extra firm tofu, diced and extra water removed with a paper towel

1 bunch kale, stems removed and cut into bite-size pieces

2 tbsp (30 ml) soy sauce, divided

2 tbsp (30 ml) water, divided

1 tbsp (15 ml) sambal

1 tbsp (15 ml) teriyaki sauce

½ cup (25 g) sliced scallions (about 3 scallions)

9 oz (255 g) soba noodles

Sesame seeds for garnish

Bring a large pot of water to a boil. In a large sauté pan, add 2 tablespoons (30 ml) of sesame oil and heat on medium-high for 1 minute. Add the tofu and spread into an even layer. Cook for 4 minutes, then turn once the first side has crisped and turned golden brown. Keep turning to brown all sides until the tofu is crispy all over, about 8 to 9 minutes total. Remove the tofu to a plate and add the remaining sesame oil.

Toss the kale in the sesame oil on medium-high heat and cook for 2 minutes. Then add 1 tablespoon (15 ml) of soy sauce and 1 tablespoon (15 ml) of water. Reduce the heat to medium and stir until all the liquid has evaporated. Repeat with the remaining 1 tablespoon (15 ml) of soy sauce and 1 tablespoon (15 ml) of water, and cook for 1 minute until the kale has softened. Add the sambal and teriyaki sauce, and stir to combine.

Return the tofu to the pan and mix it in with the sauce. Toss in the scallions. Remove from the heat.

Boil the soba noodles according to the package directions, about 4 to 5 minutes. Drain and then toss the soba with the kale and tofu. Garnish it with sesame seeds and serve warm.

SO-EASY-IT'S-SINFUL RICE AND BEAN BOWLS

SERVES 4

This is one of those meals that I can't believe I'm writing a recipe for, but it truly is one of my go-to dishes for dinner in a hurry. I always keep rice and beans in the pantry, so that means all I have to do is make sure I have the toppings we like, and a meal is essentially done. The actual cooking is negligible, so the toppings are really what make it yummy. Don't skimp on those!

Beans are a great source of fiber and folate. Remember how important folate was during your pregnancy? Guess what? It's very important when breastfeeding as well. Not only do you have increased folate needs during lactation, but two-thirds of women do not consume enough. Include beans in your diet regularly with this super simple recipe.

3 (14.5-oz [411-g]) cans black beans, rinsed and drained

1 cup (236 ml) green salsa

1 tsp cumin

½ tsp garlic powder

½ tsp smoked paprika

1 cup (210 g) jasmine rice, cooked according to package instructions

TOPPINGS
Cheddar cheese, shredded

Plum tomatoes, diced

Hass avocados, sliced

Red onion, diced

Fresh cilantro, chopped

Pickled jalapeño slices

Sour cream

Hot sauce

In a medium saucepan, add the beans, green salsa, cumin, garlic powder and paprika, and heat on medium-high for about 10 minutes, until warmed through and bubbling. You can stir the beans several times, but they don't need much attention; just mix well enough to spread the spices around. I make the rice at this time, too, since it takes just a bit longer.

To assemble, spoon the rice into a large bowl and add a generous portion of black beans. Top to your liking with cheese, tomatoes, avocado, onion, cilantro, jalapeño or sour cream. Serve with your favorite hot sauce.

SOBA NOODLE AND BROCCOLI RABE BUDDHA BOWL

SERVES 8

This is an energy-packed lunch that tastes yummy, looks pretty and is definitely picture worthy . . . go you! The bonus for kids is that noodles are fun, so they can double as a sensory activity, although my little man just likes to throw them. The bonus for parents is that you pop this in a bowl, and it'll give you the energy you need to do what you do well!

2 tbsp (30 ml) sesame oil

1 bunch broccoli rabe, chopped into 1-inch (2.5-cm) pieces and rinsed

Salt and freshly cracked pepper

1 cup (155 g) shelled edamame (found in the freezer section)

1 cup (149 g) quartered grape tomatoes

1 cup (50 g) sliced scallions (slice on the diagonal to make it prettier)

12 oz (340 g) soba noodles

SAUCE

⅓ cup (79 ml) tahini, well mixed

⅓ cup (79 ml) water (prevents the tahini from separating or becoming lumpy)

2 tbsp (29 ml) sambal (if you don't like to taste heat only use 1 tbsp [15 ml])

3 tbsp (45 ml) low-sodium soy sauce

1 tbsp (15 ml) fresh lemon juice

1 clove garlic, minced

Sesame seeds, for garnish

In a large sauté pan, add the sesame oil and cook the broccoli rabe stems and florets on high. I cook the stems and florets first, working my way from the base to the leaves, which takes less time. Once the stems have softened, about 4 minutes, add the tender leaves and cook for 1 minute, stirring constantly to make sure the leaves reach the bottom of the pan. Season with salt and pepper and remove to a large bowl.

In the same sauté pan, cook the frozen edamame with 1 tablespoon (15 ml) of water until warmed and the water evaporates, 1 to 2 minutes. Remove the edamame to the bowl with the broccoli rabe. Add the grape tomatoes and scallions to the bowl as well.

Cook the soba noodles according to package directions. Meanwhile, in a small bowl, whisk together the tahini, water, sambal, soy sauce, lemon juice and garlic. Drain the cooked soba noodles, and rinse with cold water to prevent the noodles from sticking. Drain again and then toss the noodles and sauce into your large sauté pan. Add your dressed soba noodles to the bowl with your broccoli rabe and other ingredients. Toss until well mixed and serve just warm, garnished with sesame seeds.

NOTE: Going gluten-free? Substitute rice noodles for the soba noodles and coconut aminos for the soy sauce!

ALCOHOL AND BREASTFEEDING

After sharing your body for nine months, you might be ready for a date night with your partner or maybe a date night with just a glass of wine! But is drinking alcohol safe while you are breastfeeding? The answer to that question is yes! But you have to plan carefully. First, here are a couple of things to keep in mind:

- Alcohol has been shown to affect milk production, so if you are struggling with that already, it may be best to avoid alcohol altogether.

- Alcohol passes quickly into breast milk, and the effects on your baby are related to the amount of alcohol you consume. Peak levels in breast milk occur 30 to 60 minutes after alcohol consumption but could occur up to 90 minutes later if the alcohol is consumed with food. It takes a 120-pound (55-kg) woman about 2 to 3 hours to eliminate one serving of beer, wine or spirits. "Pumping and dumping" does not accelerate the removal of alcohol from breast milk; it will continue to have alcohol in it as long as you have alcohol in your bloodstream.

If you choose to have a drink or two, you can wait for the alcohol to clear your system or make sure to have some expressed breast milk on hand. Visit www.motherisk.org to find an easy chart to follow when planning to drink while breastfeeding.

NUTRITION FOR A BREASTFEEDING MOTHER

One of the most common questions asked of registered dieticians and clinicians is "Can I lose some of this baby weight while I'm breastfeeding without it affecting my milk supply?" The answer is yes. An average-weight woman will expend 500 calories per day for the first six months if she is exclusively breastfeeding, and 400 calories per day thereafter. If you are looking to lose weight, you can consume as few as 330 calories more than your own caloric need to promote weight loss. But be careful! Decreasing your intake too much will decrease milk supply. Plan to consume at least 7 ounces (210 g) of grains, 3 cups (546 g) of vegetables, 2 cups (350 g) of fruit, 3 cups (735 g) of dairy, 6 ounces (170 g) of protein and 6 teaspoons (24 g) of fats per day. Additionally, keep in mind that you still need to drink plenty of fluids, and if you are unable to eat a varied diet or are a vegetarian or vegan, a multivitamin/multimineral supplement may be appropriate. You can customize your own lactation diet using the USDA SuperTracker at www.supertracker.usda.gov.

For those moms who lose too much weight during breastfeeding, high-fat, moderate-protein snacks like nuts, cheeses, Greek yogurt, hummus and avocados are good choices. They provide a lot of calories in a small amount of food and are nutrient dense.

BREASTFEEDING RESOURCES

WOMEN, INFANTS AND CHILDREN (WIC)

Even if you don't qualify for WIC services, there are several resources available to everyone on its website, www.fns.usda.gov/wic/breastfeeding-priority-wic-program.

LA LECHE LEAGUE

www.lllusa.org

OFFICE ON WOMEN'S HEALTH

www.womenshealth.gov/breastfeeding/breastfeeding-resources

CENTERS FOR DISEASE CONTROL AND PREVENTION (CDC)

www.cdc.gov/breastfeeding/resources/guide.htm

BREASTMILK: EVERY OUNCE COUNTS

www.breastmilkcounts.com

AMERICAN CONGRESS OF OBSTETRICIANS AND GYNECOLOGISTS

www.acog.org/About-ACOG/ACOG-Departments/Breastfeeding/Breastfeeding-Resources

FIRST FOODS

(4 TO 6 MONTHS)
PLUS RECIPES FOR USING
LEFTOVER PUREES

Introducing solids can be really exciting. First foods can get you back in the mood to cook again as you add each new fruit and vegetable to your baby's diet. Plus, if you're still breastfeeding, this may be a great time to keep up with your baby's growth without so much demand on your body.

Some babies make it easier for you to introduce solids than others. A lot is out of your control, but this doesn't have to be a stressful time where you are adding another responsibility to your already full plate. Just check out these easy recipes to get you started. Your little one will dictate the rest.

And as for those batches of purees, the chef in me had to include great ways of bringing them back to adult meals. This can be a time when your cooking energy is directed solely at your baby as you scrounge the fridge for scraps. Purees are amazing bases for soups, sauces and smoothies, so don't starve as you set out to feed your little one. Have some fun mixing it up for yourself with these recipes for leftover purees.

FIRST FOODS TIMELINE

How do you know if your baby is ready for solids? Here are some signs to look for:

- Movement of the tongue from side to side and the loss of the extrusion reflex, where babies use their tongue to thrust out any food

- Good head and trunk control

- The ability to sit well with some support

- Interest or curiosity about food

0 to 6 Months: Breast milk or iron-fortified formula is the sole source of nutrition.

6 to 8 Months: Begin with iron-fortified rice cereal and then oatmeal. Move on to smooth purees of fruits and vegetables. Because of our predisposition toward sweet foods, your baby will be more interested in fruits than in veggies. So while babies are interested in food and exploring new textures, let's get them hooked on veggies first.

After that they can have baby meats (no stringy or uncut meats) and then can move on to combination foods. At 6 to 8 months, babies begin to simulate chewing with up-and-down jaw movements. At this stage, a baby is ready for foods with a soft, lumpy texture like pureed meats, potatoes and beans.

Foods to avoid at this stage are popcorn, wheat cereals and other whole grains, raisins and whole grapes. Also avoid dried, hard raw fruits and vegetables.

8 to 12 Months: By 8 to 10 months, a baby can chew and swallow soft mashed foods like pasta and well-cooked legumes without choking. At 8 to 12 months, yogurt can be introduced with a serving size of no more than ½ cup (123 g) per day. At 12 months of age, whole milk and cheese can be added. Infants who are 9 to 12 months can eat many foods that other family members are eating such as soft-cooked vegetables, soft ripe fruits, cooked cereal, and Cheerios. Be sure to offer foods that don't require too much chewing, as these skills are not fully developed until toddlerhood.

Foods to avoid at this stage are popcorn, raisins, whole grapes and whole nuts. Also avoid dried, hard raw fruits and vegetables, and avoid difficult-to-chew fruits and vegetables (especially those with peels) as well as uncut stringy and undercooked meats and hot dog pieces served in chunks larger than ¼-inch (0.5-cm) pieces.

INTRODUCING SOLIDS: MYTHS AND FACTS

Will adding solids into a baby's diet help him or her sleep better? Unfortunately for many sleep-deprived parents, the answer to this question is no. Introducing solids too soon can be detrimental, adding unnecessary calories from carbohydrates to an infant's diet.

Do I need to offer vegetables first for my baby to like them? Healthy first foods vary among cultures and ethnic groups. Most infants prefer sweet and salty tastes and reject sour and bitter tastes. What matters most is timing and spacing.

When introducing solids, choose a single-ingredient food and offer it over three days to monitor for intolerances or allergies before introducing the next food.

FOOD SAFETY FOR INFANTS

- Remember the number 3 when determining how long food will last. Purees and other infant foods last three days in the refrigerator and three months in the freezer. Mark the containers you store them in for easy reference.

- If you are warming food in a microwave, test the food afterward and give it a good stir. Microwaves provide uneven heating and hot spots could exist. Plus, infants are a lot more sensitive to heat, so do not serve any food that feels hot or even overly warm to the touch.

- Test a new food for three days before introducing the next (this is helpful when pinpointing allergies).

- Discard any remaining food or beverage after the meal. It might be tempting to save a bit of that delicious homemade puree, but it is safest to feed out of individual portions and discard leftovers to avoid the growth of bacteria.

- Even though a baby is secured in a highchair, don't walk away during feeding. You need to watch for choking.

- After feeding a puree successfully to your baby, you can try adding a pinch of flavor from an herb or other seasoning; just don't add salt or sugar.

EQUIPMENT FOR STARTING SOLIDS

- **Bowls and utensils:** Get everything BPA-free and dishwasher and microwave safe. Look for products labeled BPA-free. If a product isn't labeled, keep in mind that some, but not all, plastics marked with recycle codes 3 or 7 may be made with BPA. It is best to use glass, porcelain or stainless-steel, instead of plastic, containers for hot foods and liquids. You will also want an assortment of baby spoons and forks. For purees, it is easiest to start with a spoon. But once your baby becomes interested in feeding him or herself and you move beyond purees, you may want to consider a fork. Not all forks are created equally, though. When the time comes, find a fork that will be easy for your child to grasp and spear food with, and look for one that has blunt tines.

- **Freezer trays and portioned containers:** BPA-free silicone trays are great for easily removing frozen purees, but in a pinch a simple ice cube tray works wonderfully. You will also want containers for storing single portions of purees in the refrigerator.

- **Washable bibs and a splash mat:** It's going to get messy, and these certainly make cleanup easy. Washable bibs are also excellent for travel because they save you a trip to the laundromat.

- **Disposable placemats:** These are great for eating at restaurants since most of your child's food will end up on the table. They also provide a safe, clean mat for your child's teethers and toys.

- **A blender:** Different options offer different benefits, but the key is to get at least one piece of equipment that purees so that no chunks remain. Baby blenders are helpful because you can work with small portions. Immersion blenders are great for easy cleanup and for soups down the road. Food processors work as well; just be sure that they puree completely. Standard blenders are also good; you may just need to make more puree at once and freeze the leftovers.

- **A potato ricer:** This is a wonderful addition to the kitchen, and you can't do better for mashed potatoes.

- **A medium-size stockpot with a lid and steamer basket.** This will be used for all your steamed vegetables and early cooked purees.

- **A vegetable scrub brush and peeler.** You will want to thoroughly clean all fruits and vegetables before serving them to your baby. These simple tools are kitchen essentials for that task.

NO-COOK FIRST FOODS

There are some great first foods that require no cooking at all! Just be sure to wash all fruits and vegetables before cutting. The steps for making the purees below are as simple as wash, peel, pit (if needed) and puree.

- Apricot

- Avocado

- Banana

- Mango

- Nectarine

- Papaya

- Peach

GRANDMA'S EFFORTLESS APPLESAUCE

MAKES 4 CUPS (946 ML)

Apples are a great first food for a baby. They are highly unlikely to cause an allergic reaction and have a texture that keeps a baby interested.

This was the first puree my son gobbled up with glee. My earlier attempt with homemade rice cereal was snubbed, but Grandma's easy applesauce got that first smile as my son licked every sweet drop off his spoon. I still make this almost once a week. It is easy to mix it up by changing the spices, say cinnamon one week and ginger the next. Once your baby is on to combination foods, you can add carrots, spinach or even kale. With applesauce, the combinations are endless.

6 cups (720 g) peeled, cored and roughly chopped apples (about 5 medium apples)

1¼ cups (295 ml) water

1 tsp ground cinnamon, optional

In a medium-size stockpot with a lid, add your apples and water. Cover and bring to a boil, turn down the heat to medium and continue to cook covered until the apples are soft to the touch, about 10 minutes. Puree the apples and remaining water with an immersion blender. You can also use a blender, but the immersion blender really does save some steps in cleanup. Cool, then refrigerate or freeze in portions.

THE BEST APPLE VARIETIES FOR APPLESAUCE:
Fuji
Gala
Golden Delicious
Honeycrisp
Pink Lady

APPLE, CARROT AND GINGER MUFFINS

MAKES 12 MUFFINS

This is a tasty, healthy breakfast for parents and tots alike. Apple puree is a wonderful substitution for refined sugar in baking and helps make recipes a little healthier and definitely more baby friendly. For toddlers, these muffins are a great way to add fiber and vegetables. Best is that one batch gives you breakfast on the go for almost a full workweek.

1 cup (120 g) whole wheat flour

1 cup (125 g) all-purpose flour

1 tsp baking soda

1 tsp baking powder

½ tsp cinnamon

¼ tsp salt

¾ cup (178 ml) almond milk

¼ cup (59 ml) melted butter

¾ cup (150 g) brown sugar

2 eggs

1 cup (236 ml) applesauce

1 tsp grated fresh ginger (1-inch [2.5-cm] piece)

1 cup (110 g) grated carrots

Preheat your oven to 400°F (204°C).

Place the whole wheat and all-purpose flours, baking soda, baking powder, cinnamon and salt in a large mixing bowl. Whisk together until well mixed.

In a medium bowl, combine the almond milk, butter, brown sugar, eggs, applesauce, ginger and carrots.

Fold the wet ingredients into the dry ingredients with a large spatula until just combined. You don't want to overwork the flour, so mix just until you no longer see flour.

Spoon the muffin batter into greased muffin tins or muffin tins with wrappers in them. Fill three-quarters full to allow for the muffins to rise. Bake for 20 minutes or until an inserted toothpick comes out clean. Cool on a wire rack and serve at room temperature.

NOTE: These muffins keep great overnight when left on a wire rack, covered with a clean dishcloth. Alternately, they can keep up to four days in an airtight container. Just be sure to allow the muffins to cool completely, then line the container with paper towels to keep the muffins from getting soggy.

PEAR PUREE

MAKES 2 CUPS (473 ML)

Pear purees are sweeter than apple and even quicker to make. I like to use them in combination with greens that might otherwise be less appealing. Kale and pear is one of my favorite combinations. This puree is also a great sugar substitute in baking.

---

3 cups (480 g) peeled, cored and chopped ripe pears (3 pears)

½ cup (120 ml) water

¼ tsp ginger powder, optional

In a medium saucepan with a lid, add the pears and water, cover and bring to a boil. Reduce to medium heat and cook, covered, for 8 minutes, until the pears have softened.

Puree the pears and remaining water with an immersion blender until smooth, then mix in the ginger. Cool, then refrigerate or freeze in portions.

PEAR AND OAT SMOOTHIE

SERVES 2

Smoothies are the perfect use for leftover fruit purees. They are incredibly easy and are the fastest breakfast I've found, which is great if you're not a morning person (I am not). This smoothie tastes pretty much like a creamy pear tart. It is soft on the stomach and solves the dilemma of breakfast for parents in a hurry.

¼ cup (23 g) oats

1 cup (237 ml) Pear Puree (page 100)

¼ cup (59 ml) full-fat Greek yogurt

1 cup (237 ml) unsweetened vanilla almond milk (substitute whole milk or a scoop of protein powder to increase your protein intake)

¼ tsp cinnamon

1 tsp freshly grated ginger

Puree the oats in a food processor or blender until they form a powder. You really want to grind them fine, otherwise you will get flecks of oat in the finished smoothie.

Add the Pear Puree, yogurt, almond milk, cinnamon and ginger, and puree until smooth.

BUTTERNUT SQUASH PUREE

MAKES ABOUT 5½ CUPS (1 L) DEPENDING ON THE SIZE OF THE SQUASH

Butternut squash is an amazing first food that is made even more delicious through the process of roasting, which gives the squash its caramelized flavor.

Whenever I'm roasting vegetables, I make sure to have several sheets going since the oven is already on and it's great to have extra veggies to snack on. With the ingredients for this puree, I'd also roast a bunch of sweet potatoes for Sweet Potato Puree (page 112). That way the same amount of cook time gets you double the results.

---

1 small butternut squash

1 tbsp (15 ml) olive oil

2½ cups (592 ml) water

Preheat your oven to 400°F (204°C).

Line a baking sheet with aluminum foil. Slice your butternut squash in half, and scoop out and discard the seeds. Spread the olive oil on the inside of both halves of the squash, and roast them skin side up for 45 minutes. Allow to cool, then scoop out the filling with a spoon.

In a strong blender, blend the filling with the water until the puree is completely smooth. Cool, then refrigerate or freeze in portions.

BUTTERNUT SQUASH MAC 'N' CHEESE

SERVES 8 TO 10

This recipe is full of calcium. The ideal family meal, it is incredibly infant and toddler friendly. If your toddler has rejected milk, this is a great dish to help meet your little one's calcium needs. It also makes for a perfect option during teething since it is soft and comforting.

Below are two versions, one made from puree and one if you are cooking your squash from scratch.

1 tbsp (14 g) butter, softened

2 lbs (908 g) pasta (I chose penne)

4 cups (820 g) peeled, seeded and diced butternut squash (about 1 small butternut squash), or substitute 5 cups (1.2 L) Butternut Squash Puree (page 104)

2 cups (480 ml) chicken stock (omit if using puree)

2 tsp (10 ml) Dijon mustard

2 cups (216 g) grated Gruyere cheese, or substitute equal parts cheddar

2 cups (242 g) grated cheddar cheese

1 cup (237 ml) whole milk

¾ cup (180 ml) Greek yogurt

Sea salt and freshly cracked pepper

TOPPINGS

2 tbsp (30 ml) melted butter

1 cup (121 g) grated cheddar cheese

1 cup (108 g) panko bread crumbs

Preheat your oven to 400°F (204°C).

Grease two 8 x 8-inch (20.5 × 20.5-cm) baking dishes with butter. In a large pot, bring salted water to a boil and cook the pasta according to package instructions.

To make the squash from scratch, in a medium stockpot, bring the squash and stock to a boil. Cover and cook for 15 minutes, until the squash is tender. Use an immersion blender to puree the squash and stock mixture until it is completely smooth.

Remove the pureed squash from the heat and add the mustard and Gruyere and cheddar cheeses. Stir until melted.

If you're starting with the premade puree, warm it in a large pot until hot enough for the cheeses to melt when they're stirred in, add the cheese and then remove from the heat.

Add the milk and Greek yogurt to the finished pureed squash (whether freshly made or from a premade puree). From this point the two recipes are the same.

Stir your creamy base until smooth and then season with salt and pepper.

Toss the pasta with the squash and cheese sauce in the large pot. Mix thoroughly and use a spatula to spoon it into the prepared baking dishes.

In a small bowl, mix the melted butter, cheddar cheese and bread crumbs, then sprinkle it over the top. Bake for 20 to 25 minutes, until bubbling. Serve warm.

CARROT PUREE

MAKES 3 CUPS (710 ML)

You have probably heard that carrots are good for your vision, but these little nutrition powerhouses have so much more to offer. Carrots are a good source of several B vitamins, vitamin K, potassium and other plant compounds with numerous health benefits; all great reasons for starting with this easy puree.

My son loved carrot puree. If you pick a nice bunch of carrots, this puree will burst with wonderfully sweet flavor. It's a very gentle starter food that is also great when mixed with other fresh fruits and vegetables once you begin combination foods.

2½ cups (320 g) peeled and chopped carrots (1 large bunch)

2¼ cups (533 ml) water

In a medium stockpot, add the carrots and water. Bring to a boil and then cover and reduce the heat to medium. Cook for 25 to 30 minutes, until the carrots are tender. Cool the carrots, and then puree them with any remaining water in a blender or food processor until smooth. Refrigerate or freeze in portions.

CARROT CUMIN SOUP

SERVES 4

I've always loved a creamy vegetable soup. This is the perfect recipe for using Carrot Puree (page 108). It makes a great hot lunch and is the perfect starting course for a fall dinner.

Need one more reason to try this soup? Carrots can aid in weight loss! Research has shown that when used as a part of a meal, carrots can increase the feeling of fullness and decrease calorie intake in future meals.

1 tbsp (15 ml) olive oil

½ cup (76 g) finely chopped onion

1 clove garlic, minced

1 tbsp (10 g) cumin

2½ cups (600 ml) Carrot Puree (page 108)

1 (13.5-oz [400-ml]) can full-fat coconut milk

Sea salt and freshly cracked pepper

TOPPINGS

Greek yogurt (full fat)

Toasted pumpkin seeds

Fresh cilantro leaves

Add olive oil to a medium-size stockpot over medium heat. Add the onion and garlic, and sauté for 3 to 5 minutes, until softened and translucent, being careful not to brown. Stir in the cumin until the onions are coated, then transfer to a blender with the Carrot Puree. Puree until the onions are as smooth as the rest of the puree, then transfer back to the stockpot. Bring the mixture to a boil, then reduce the heat to low and stir in the coconut milk. Heat until warmed through and season to taste with salt and pepper.

Serve the soup hot, topped with yogurt, pumpkin seeds and cilantro. This soup is also good as is without toppings.

SWEET POTATO PUREE

MAKES 5 CUPS (1 L)

The roasting helps caramelize the sweet potatoes and makes them extra delicious. This puree mixes very well with meats later down the road once you begin combination purees with your child.

2 medium to large sweet potatoes

1¼ cups (296 ml) water

Preheat your oven to 400°F (204°C).

Line a baking sheet with aluminum foil. Prick the sweet potatoes several times on both sides and bake on the sheet for 45 minutes. Allow to cool then remove the skin and puree in a blender adding water slowly, until completely smooth. (If you're using smaller sweet potatoes, use less water.) Freeze in individual portions or allow to cool before serving.

SOUTHWEST SWEET POTATO CAKES AND BLACK BEAN SALSA FRESCA

MAKES 12 CAKES

Vegetable cakes are a great way to get your kids, or yourself, to eat more vegetables. My parents used to make us corn fritters, and I've always had a soft spot for latkes. These cakes are perfect for leftover mashed sweet potatoes and pair perfectly with Black Bean Salsa Fresca to make them a more substantial meal.

Nervous about the butter in this recipe? Don't be! Fat-soluble vitamins (A, D, E and K) are absorbed better when consumed with fat. And since sweet potatoes are packed with vitamins, let's make the most of them!

BLACK BEAN SALSA FRESCA

2 cups (320 g) small diced plum tomatoes (4 plum tomatoes)

½ cup (80 g) finely diced red onion

1½ limes, juiced

1 small jalapeño, seeded, deveined and minced, optional

1 cup (16 g) cilantro leaves, chopped

½ tsp salt

1 tbsp (15 ml) olive oil

1 clove garlic, minced

½ cup (90 g) black beans

SOUTHWEST SWEET POTATO CAKES

2½ cups (637 g) mashed sweet potatoes (2 large sweet potatoes)

½ cup (62 g) all-purpose flour

¼ cup (12 g) sliced scallions (2 large scallions)

¼ tsp smoked paprika

¼ tsp cumin

¼ cup (30 g) grated cheddar cheese

4 tbsp (57 g) butter for frying, divided

TO MAKE THE BLACK BEAN SALSA FRESCA

In a medium bowl, combine all the ingredients and stir until mixed. As this salsa sits, the tomato juice makes it a bit watery. For easiest serving, drain with a slotted spoon before adding to the sweet potato cakes. Set aside or refrigerate until ready to serve.

TO MAKE THE SOUTHWEST SWEET POTATO CAKES

In a large bowl, mix the sweet potatoes, flour, scallions, paprika, cumin and cheese together. Stir until well combined. Add 2 tablespoons (28 g) of butter to a large frying pan and heat until melted. Using wet hands, take a spoonful of sweet potato batter and pat into a thin, 3- to 4-inch (7.5- to 10-cm) diameter disc. It doesn't have to be perfect. The batter will be a little sticky. You can spoon the batter into the pan and use a fork to mash it down. But it is important to keep it thin. Work in batches to prevent overcrowding.

Fry the cakes for 2 to 3 minutes per side on high until they're a deep golden brown. The cheese may cause them to stick a little to the pan, so use a nonstick pan and plenty of butter.

Remove the cooked cakes to a plate and repeat with the batter until all the cakes are cooked. Serve warm with Black Bean Salsa Fresca.

MANGO PUREE

MAKES 1½ CUPS (355 ML)

Yellow mango is so sweet and delicious that it is sure to be an instant favorite with your child. The bonus with yellow mangoes is that they are often much less stringy than other mangoes, making them much easier to puree. Make sure your mangoes are just soft to the touch with no bruises or soft spots.

---

2 yellow mangoes

Wash your mangoes and slice them lengthwise against the pit, yielding two large halves around the long, narrow pit. Slice each half into quarters and use a knife to cut the peel away. Roughly dice the remaining fruit. Use your knife to cut any remaining fruit off the pit.

In a blender, puree the fruit until smooth.

NOTE: This puree makes the ultimate smoothie base and also mixes well with greens and other fruits once your infant moves on to combinations.

MANGO SORBET

SERVES 4

I'm not sure how many parents are going to make sorbet with leftover fruit purees but what a killer recipe to have in your back pocket. Especially if you ever go fruit picking or fall upon a stash of perfectly ripe peaches, raspberries or mangoes, the effort is well worth it. This recipe is for occasions when you want to feel special and capable and possibly daring enough to invite friends over for dinner and wow them with a palate cleanser. I'm talking the stuff of wonderful daydreams.

Since I don't have an ice cream maker, this is a recipe for getting around that step. It is basically in the book because I think it's really cool, and if you make your own sorbet even once in your lifetime, I think you'll still pat yourself on the back and feel like you've walked on the moon.

---

2 ripe mangoes, peeled, skinned and pitted

¼ cup (50 g) white sugar

½ tsp lime juice

Pinch of salt

2 tbsp (30 ml) water

Puree the mango in a small food processor or blender until completely smooth. Pass the mango puree through a fine-mesh sieve into a medium bowl, scraping with a spatula as you go. This is a slightly fussy step but really keeps the texture of your sorbet very silky and makes sure no threads of mango pulp ruin an otherwise delectable dessert.

Whisk in the sugar, lime juice, salt and water, then pour the mixture onto a parchment-lined baking sheet and freeze until set, about 2 hours.

To serve, blend once more. If your mixture is not blending well, add additional cold water bit by bit as needed until you reach your desired consistency. Sorbet should spoon easily and be very creamy when tasted.

THE DIRTY DOZEN AND CLEAN 15

Should you feed your baby only organic foods? This is a frequently asked question. The bottom line is this: The label "organic" is a production claim, not a nutrition claim. Numerous studies have shown that there is no difference nutritionally between organic and conventionally produced foods. Organic produce is grown without the use of pesticides, synthetic fertilizers, sewage sludge, GMOs or ionizing radiation. Organic meat, poultry, eggs and dairy come from animals that were not treated with antibiotics or growth hormones. If you want to limit the amount of pesticides your family consumes, you can use The Dirty Dozen and Clean 15 lists provided by the Environmental Working Group (www.ewg.org) when you head to the grocery store.

The Dirty Dozen and Clean 15 help consumers know when to buy organic foods based on a pesticide residue ranking system. The Dirty Dozen are the fruits and vegetables with the highest amounts of potential contaminants, so buying organic is the way to go when possible. The Clean 15 have little to no traces of contaminants, so you can purchase nonorganic options.

THE DIRTY DOZEN (AS OF 2017)

1. Strawberries

2. Spinach

3. Nectarines

4. Apples

5. Peaches

6. Pears

7. Cherries

8. Grapes

9. Celery

10. Tomatoes

11. Sweet bell peppers as well as hot peppers

12. Potatoes

THE CLEAN 15 (AS OF 2017)

1. Sweet corn

2. Avocados

3. Pineapple

4. Cabbage

5. Onions

6. Frozen sweet peas

7. Papayas

8. Asparagus

9. Mangoes

10. Eggplant

11. Honeydew

12. Kiwi

13. Cantaloupe

14. Cauliflower

15. Grapefruit

PORTION SIZES FOR BABIES AND TODDLERS

Portion sizes for infants beginning to eat solids vary from infant to infant. First meals will be small, maybe five to six spoonfuls, and last about 10 minutes depending on your baby's attention span. A tablespoon of food at a meal is perfectly normal during infancy. Remember, breast milk or formula are still your baby's main source of nutrition during the majority of the first 12 months. Don't get too hung up on portion size; instead look for cues your baby is giving you. When your baby is full, he or she may start to play with the food or spoon, slow the pace of eating and refuse or spit out food.

TIPS FOR COOKING WITH AND FEEDING A 6-MONTH-OLD

- Use old burp cloths for cleanup after meals. Wet them slightly with warm water, and they make the perfect washcloth (they will be much softer than paper towels or wet wipes, and your child shouldn't mind their soft texture).

- Preload the spoon so that a flavor your child loves is at the front and a new food you're trying is right behind it.

- Bath toys make great high chair distractions and are made to get wet and to clean easily.

- Kitchen utensils such as a whisk, plastic measuring spoons, plastic storage containers and a salad spinner make fun distractions for a child to play with as you cook.

- Set up a bouncer or pack and play in the kitchen so your baby is safely contained but can enjoy watching you cook.

COMBINATION FOODS
(6 TO 8 MONTHS)

As you work your way through first foods and into combinations, your little one's world opens up. Soon your refrigerator and freezer begin to look like a colorful rainbow of pureed fruits and vegetables. Here's where you get to play mixologist. You can start to work in a greater variety of vegetables that may be harder for babies to love on their own but are delightful to babies once mixed with a little apple or pear puree.

INTRODUCING WATER

Breast milk or formula provides a baby's fluid needs for the first 6 months. Infants aged 7 to 12 months need 27 ounces (800 ml) of fluid per day. This fluid can be provided by breast milk, formula, foods and water.

Readiness to drink from a cup begins at 6 to 8 months of age. This is a good time to introduce water. The typical portion size for introducing water is 1 to 2 ounces (29 to 57 ml). You should offer this amount each time your baby has a meal as well as between meals, especially during warm months.

NOTE: Juice is not required to meet your baby's fluid needs. In fact, juice and other sugar-containing beverages can promote cavities. If juice is offered, it should be after 6 months of age and never in a bottle. This is a great time to help your baby develop a preference for water, so delaying the introduction of juice helps during this milestone.

BABY GUACAMOLE

MAKES ½ CUP (118 ML)

Avocados deliver healthy fats, and infants are at high risk for essential fatty acid deficiency because of their accelerated growth.

Another reason to make this delicious puree is that it is a wonderful way to add greens to a child's diet. This recipe is great as a puree or as a dip or sauce for toddler meals. The portion size is small because, honestly, it takes a minute to make and an avocado is always freshest when eaten immediately.

½ Hass avocado

1 tbsp (10 g) defrosted chopped frozen spinach (I buy organic)

In a small blender or food processor, combine the avocado and spinach, and blend until smooth. You can also simply mash the avocado and stir in the spinach. Just be sure to mince the spinach with a knife beforehand so that it is in very fine pieces that easily blend into the creamy avocado.

NOTE: For toddlers, I often add slightly warmed rice to this puree to make a delicious side dish for meals.

NOTE: After 8 months or when your pediatrician has added yogurt to your child's diet, you can add 1 tablespoon (15 ml) of plain yogurt to make this guacamole an even creamier sauce for babies and toddlers.

APPLE, SWEET POTATO AND CORN PUREE

MAKES 2¼ CUPS (533 ML)

This puree was one of my son's favorites when we moved on to combinations. The sweet corn adds fiber, a little protein, B vitamins and potassium. This recipe also includes sweet potatoes and apples, making an easy and appetizing puree of three naturally sweet ingredients.

1 cup (133 g) peeled and diced sweet potato

1 cup (110 g) peeled, seeded and diced apple

1½ cups (355 ml) water

¼ cup (41 g) frozen sweet corn

Combine the sweet potato and apple in a medium stockpot, and add the water. Bring to a boil and then cover and reduce the heat to medium. Cook for 20 to 25 minutes, until the sweet potato falls apart when tested with a fork. In the last 5 minutes of cooking, add the sweet corn.

Cool and then puree the mixture in a blender or food processor until smooth. Store in the refrigerator or freeze in portions for later use.

PEAR, KIWI AND SPINACH PUREE

MAKES 1¼ CUPS (296 ML)

This is the most amazing smoothie base as well as a wonderfully vibrant and healthy puree for baby. Spinach is an excellent addition to any puree. It adds a multitude of vitamins and minerals, including iron, and is low in calories, making it a nutrient-dense food.

1 pear, peeled and cored

3 tbsp (45 ml) water

½ cup (78 g) frozen chopped spinach (I use organic)

1 kiwi, skin and tough center removed

In a small stockpot, add the pear and water, and bring to a light boil. Reduce the heat to medium, cover and cook for 8 minutes, until the pear has softened. Add the spinach and cool. Puree with the kiwi until completely smooth.

PUMPKIN, APPLE AND CARROT PUREE

MAKES 1½ CUPS (355 ML)

This simple recipe will easily please an early eater. It is all the best flavors of the fall harvest in a spoon.

½ cup (64 g) peeled and finely chopped carrots

1 cup (110 g) peeled, seeded and diced apple

1 cup (237 ml) water

¼ cup (60 ml) canned 100% pure pumpkin

In a medium stockpot, combine the carrots and apple with water, cover and bring to a boil. Reduce the heat to medium, and cook covered for 20 minutes, until the carrots are soft.

Puree the apple, carrots and water mixture with the pumpkin in a food processor or blender until smooth. If you want a thinner puree, add additional water 1 tablespoon (15 ml) at a time to reach the desired consistency. Serve when cool or freeze individual portions for later use.

VERY BERRY PUREE

MAKES 1¼ CUPS (296 ML)

This puree is vibrant in color and incredibly versatile to use in meals. Berries are a low-sugar fruit and are filled with fiber. Blueberries are actually considered a superfood because of their antioxidant and phytochemical makeup. Superfood for a super baby!

This puree is great on its own, served with oatmeal or yogurt, or even made into popsicles.

---

1 cup (83 g) strawberries, stems removed

½ cup (62 g) raspberries

½ cup (74 g) blueberries

Wash the strawberries, raspberries and blueberries thoroughly, then puree in a blender until smooth.

NOTE: If you want to change the consistency, add banana to make the puree more easily spoonable and slightly sweeter for a child hesitant about berries.

VERY BERRY COCONUT POPSICLES

MAKES 8 TO 10 POPSICLES

If you have a kid, it is worth it to get your own popsicle molds. They are affordable and offer countless opportunities for fun and experimentation. When I was young, my parents used to make my brother and me a lot of popsicles. They're a summer staple, and it is nice to be able to make your own without scouring the stores for ones without a ton of added sugar. Plus, if you're still breastfeeding, I can't think of a more refreshing snack.

1 (13.5-oz [400-ml]) can unsweetened full-fat coconut milk

1 tsp vanilla extract

3 tbsp (45 ml) honey

1 cup (240 ml) Very Berry Puree (page 132), or any blended fruit puree

In a large mixing bowl with a spout, whisk the coconut milk, vanilla and honey until combined. Fill the popsicle molds to 2 inches (5 cm). Add the popsicle sticks and freeze for 10 minutes to create a base.

Take the molds out of the freezer, and finish filling them by alternating with the Very Berry Puree and the remaining coconut milk mixture using a wooden skewer to swirl and create a pattern. If you don't feel like the fuss of a swirl, you can blend the puree and coconut together from the beginning. Once you've filled your molds, freeze the popsicles until they're set, 4 hours to overnight.

To eat the popsicles, run the mold under hot water for several seconds so the popsicles are easy to remove from the mold. Savor each delicious bite!

NOTE: You can substitute your favorite fruit puree for the Very Berry Puree. Other combinations that are wickedly delicious are mango and coconut, orange and coconut, strawberry and coconut, pineapple and coconut, blackberry and coconut and raspberry and coconut.

PEA, POTATO AND LEEK PUREE

MAKES ABOUT 6 CUPS (1.5 L)

This is a filling combination that your baby can enjoy either as a thick puree or,
as Mommy and Daddy might have it, as a soup.

1 cup (89 g) diced leeks

1 tbsp (14 g) butter

2 cups (300 g) peeled and diced
Idaho potatoes

2 cups (300 g) frozen peas

2 cups (473 ml) chicken stock

In a medium stockpot, sauté the leeks in the butter for 5 to 7 minutes, until softened. Add the potatoes, peas and chicken stock, and bring to a boil. Cover and cook for 12 to 15 minutes at a medium boil. Test the potatoes with a fork, and once they fall apart when tested, they're done.

Puree until smooth with an immersion blender. This does make the potatoes a bit glutinous. If that bothers your little one, try mashing the vegetables with a potato masher or potato ricer. Make sure that pea husks blend fully, since that is something that often triggers an adverse reaction from a baby. Cool before serving or storing for later use.

PEA, POTATO AND LEEK SOUP

SERVES 6 TO 8

This is a flavor-packed pea soup that is a wonderful use of the Pea, Potato and Leek Puree (page 136). This soup is delicious paired with your child's favorite cheddar crackers, whether they take the shape of fish, rockets or bunnies. Just don't let them catch you swiping their snacks!

6 cups (1.5 L) Pea, Potato and Leek Puree (page 136)

2 cups (473 ml) chicken stock

½ tsp garlic powder

2 tbsp (8 g) minced fresh parsley

½ cup (118 ml) heavy cream

Sea salt and freshly cracked pepper

Crusty bread for dipping

TOPPINGS

Greek yogurt

Sweet peas

Add the Pea, Potato and Leek Puree to a large stockpot. Mix in the stock, garlic powder and parsley, and bring to a boil. Reduce the heat to low. Stir until the stock fully blends with the puree and forms a silky-smooth soup.

Remove from the heat once fully mixed, and stir in the heavy cream. Season to taste with salt and pepper.

Ladle into bowls and garnish with a swirl of Greek yogurt and a sprinkling of peas. Serve with crusty bread for dipping.

CREAMED CORN AND CHICKEN CASSEROLE

MAKES 1¾ CUPS (414 ML)

For an infant ready to try meat for the first time, this is a wonderful puree. Many babies and even toddlers reject meat because of its unique texture. Pureeing it with corn gives it a more acceptable texture and a sweet taste a baby is sure to gobble up.

1 tbsp (15 ml) olive oil

1 chicken breast tender (or ½ cup [70 g] cooked chicken)

½ cup (82 g) frozen sweet corn

¼ cup (32 g) finely chopped carrots

1 cup (236 ml) chicken stock

Pinch of dried thyme

½ cup (81 g) cooked jasmine rice

In a sauté pan with a lid, add the olive oil and chicken, and cook the chicken on medium heat for 5 to 7 minutes, until cooked through. Test to make sure no pink remains when sliced with a knife. Set aside on a plate.

Add the corn, carrots, stock and thyme to the pan. Bring the mixture to a boil, and then cover and reduce the heat to medium. Cook for about 20 minutes, until the carrots are tender when tested.

In a small blender or food processor, blend the chicken and corn mixture with the rice until smooth. Allow to cool before serving, or freeze in individual portions for later use.

FOOD ALLERGIES

Infants develop their immune systems over a few years, and their GI tracts are sensitive compared to those of older children. This can make it difficult to identify an allergy, intolerance or sensitivity. True food allergies are more frequent in younger children, but only about 6 to 8 percent of children under 4 have allergies that started in infancy. In other words, allergies in infants are relatively rare. The most common allergic reactions are difficulty breathing and skin problems. Food intolerances are often suspected in infants.

There are eight foods that make up 90 percent of food allergies:

1. Eggs

2. Milk

3. Peanuts

4. Tree nuts

5. Fish

6. Shellfish

7. Wheat

8. Soy

Families often chalk up rashes, congestion, diarrhea and gas to a food intolerance, but in most cases they are not due to a food intolerance at all. Remember the developing immune system? The National Institutes of Health does not recommend preventing food allergies by avoiding or delaying the introduction of specific foods thought to cause allergies. In fact, avoiding or restricting food can lead to poor nutrition and a limited variety in your child's diet.

The good news is that children allergic to milk or eggs have a good chance of growing out of the allergy.

NOTE: Allergy and intolerance symptoms are more common in response to nonfood items like grass and dust. However, if you do suspect a food allergy, see an allergist, who will be able to make a diagnosis. If your family has a history of food allergies, talk with your pediatrician before introducing these foods to your child so you can create a plan for how to do so. If your child has a serious reaction to a food item, call 911 immediately.

TIPS FOR PICKY EATERS

- Keep reintroducing the same food to your baby even if the first reaction is not enthusiastic. It can take 10 to 15 times before a food is accepted by your infant. Just be sure to always offer some options that your infant loves at each meal to keep the dining experience enjoyable.

- Don't force food. If your infant doesn't want to eat or is averse to a certain food, don't sneak spoonfuls. You don't want to frustrate your child or make eating unpleasant.

- One trick is to preload a spoon so that at the front is a favorite food and at the back is something new. Sometimes after that first accepted bite, feeding can go smoothly. Popular front loaders are applesauce or yogurt.

- Let your baby have his or her own spoon. Simply having control of the spoon can help your child be a more active and happier participant at meals.

- Always offer options at mealtime but never more than a few. This empowers but doesn't overwhelm young diners.

- Once you move on to finger foods, cut food into fun shapes using cookie cutters. Pasta is also a great option for experimenting with shapes.

- Keep your baby from snacking a lot before meals.

- Smoothies and sauces are a great way to add vegetables to a young child's diet. Check out the Mommy and Me Green Smoothies (page 168) for a great way to add spinach.

- When possible, eat your meals together as a family; it is helpful when your child sees you eating the same food. This makes them more willing to try new foods. Having a positive food environment (not calling foods gross, yucky, etc.) is conducive to a varied diet.

- Offer a healthy favorite food at each meal. This way your child will see a favorite before they even begin eating that will get them excited for meals.

- Make meals in advance and have food handy for young eaters. You don't want to start cooking when your child is already ready to eat.

EXPANDING TASTES
(8 TO 10 MONTHS)

At this stage, your baby probably has his or her first tooth. You can begin to add some soft chunks to your purees. Some children move quickly to textured food, while others still enjoy purees, so the recipes in this chapter reflect both those desires. Also, this is the stage you can add yogurt (a favorite of many infants) to your baby's diet. Then there's meat. As an omnivorous family, we enjoyed adding meat to my son's meals. The added protein helped satisfy his appetite and seemed to help him sleep longer and deeper.

Your child can enjoy almost the full spectrum of foods the family is eating at this point. Just consult your pediatrician as you close the gap on those final foods to get your tot table ready.

INTRODUCING DAIRY

According to the American Academy of Pediatrics, dairy foods should not be introduced before 8 months of age. At 8 to 12 months, yogurt can be introduced with a serving size of no more than a half cup (118 ml) per day, and at 12 months of age, whole milk and cheese can be added. The cheese in White Bean, Pumpkin and Kale Puree (page 152), Rinkle's Risotto (page 156) and Butternut Squash Puree (page 104) are fine after 8 months. Cheese can be part of a recipe; some pediatricians just recommend holding off on giving cheese by itself because of its unique texture. At 12 months, six servings of dairy is recommended, with a serving being a half cup (118 ml) of yogurt, a half cup (118 ml) of milk and a half ounce (14 g) of cheese.

Dairy products have become a bit controversial these days. Some groups tout the benefits of dairy and others abhor it. So what's a parent to do? Don't be afraid of dairy. Dairy has a great nutrient profile, including calcium, vitamin D, riboflavin, B12, potassium and phosphorus. When possible, choose full-fat, organic products that come from cows that are grass fed and raised in a pasture.

STOP AND GO FOODS

STOP: When you want to stop constant movements (diarrhea) you can continue your baby's normal feedings with the addition of extra fluids, including an electrolyte-replacement beverage (in most cases). Stay away from foods with simple sugars as this may make diarrhea worse. Some foods to try are carbohydrates like rice, bread, potato, pasta and baby cereal (avoiding whole grains). Also, banana, applesauce, carrots and yogurt may help your infant. If your baby becomes dehydrated or less responsive than normal, seek medical attention.

GO: Also common and usually short-lived in childhood, constipation can be a problem with young children. Focus on fluid intake and increasing fiber, but be careful as many high-fiber foods present choking hazards. Use the stage of food your child is ingesting whether it is pureed, softly mashed or soft, chewable chunks.

Some high-fiber foods to offer are high-fiber pastas, Brussels sprouts, spinach, broccoli, peas and beans. If your baby is older than 6 months, you can offer 2 to 4 ounces (59 to 118 ml) of prune juice. This works even better if the prune juice is warmed; just be careful that it's not hot (remember, infants have a greater sensitivity to heat). Fruits to try are pears, prunes and apricots. It is also good to try to offer more water.

Currently, there is not enough evidence to support the use of probiotics and prebiotics for diarrhea or constipation in infants and children. Additionally, the long-term effects of probiotic use on a child's GI tract are unknown.

VERY BERRY OATMEAL BREAKFAST

SERVES 1

This is your baby's first parfait, and it has all the best flavors of the morning swirled together. Oatmeal is a good recipe to have in your back pocket. When my son moved beyond oatmeal cereal to actual oatmeal, I could make breakfast for the whole family in a snap. I love oatmeal in the cool-weather months and often make it in advance since it is so easy to rewarm. It is a healthy and easy breakfast that can be adapted a thousand ways. The Very Berry Oatmeal Breakfast is just one of those ways.

FOR THE OATMEAL

2 cups (473 ml) water

1 cup (90 g) old-fashioned rolled oats

FOR THE PARFAIT

1 tbsp (15 ml) Very Berry Puree (page 132), or other fruit puree

1 tbsp (15 ml) plain yogurt

TO MAKE THE OATMEAL

In a medium stockpot, bring the water to a boil and stir in the oats. Return to a boil and then simmer for 5 to 10 minutes until the water is absorbed and the oats are the way you like them. For a small child, I always err on the side of softness. Test them, and when they no longer have crunch or bite, they are ready. You can also puree the finished oatmeal if your child is still fond of smoother textures. Set aside to cool.

TO ASSEMBLE A SERVING OF VERY BERRY OATMEAL BREAKFAST

Mix ¼ cup (20 g) of slightly warmed or room temperature oatmeal with a swirl of Very Berry Puree and a swirl of yogurt. You can get beautiful with your designs, or you can mix all the ingredients together into a pretty, light-pink porridge. It is up to you how you serve it. No matter what, the flavors blend nicely.

VARIATIONS

Switch up your Very Berry Puree for Grandma's Effortless Applesauce (page 96) or Pear Puree (page 100). Peach puree or cherry puree are also good substitutions. Basically, any flavor that sounds good for pie is perfect for this meal.

BANANA RICE PUDDING

1 SERVING

This recipe follows the BRAT diet, which includes bananas, rice, applesauce and toast. It is a wonderful baby comfort food for when your infant's digestion is off. The idea behind the BRAT diet is that it provides some "tummy rest" and is low in fiber, protein and fat. So use this simple recipe for comfort or as a yummy snack in addition to mealtime. Just don't make it in advance because your bananas will turn brown.

½ ripe banana, mashed

1 tsp yogurt

Dash of cinnamon

1 tbsp (10 g) cooked jasmine rice

In a small glass bowl, mix the banana, yogurt, cinnamon and rice together until smooth.

WHITE BEAN, PUMPKIN AND KALE PUREE

MAKES ABOUT 1 CUP (244 ML)

Here is a vegetarian puree packed with flavor and protein. Pumpkin is a nutrition powerhouse! It is a good source of fiber, vitamin A, vitamin C, riboflavin and potassium. This recipe tastes much like a white bean and kale soup with the added benefit of pumpkin.

½ cup (34 g) chopped fresh kale

1 tsp olive oil

½ cup (118 ml) vegetable stock

¼ cup (45 g) rinsed canned white beans

¼ cup (60 ml) canned 100% pumpkin

2 tbsp (20 g) white rice

1 tbsp (11 g) grated Parmesan cheese

In a medium-size stockpot over medium heat, sauté the kale in olive oil for 3 minutes, stirring several times until it begins to soften. Add the stock, white beans and pumpkin to the pot. Stir to combine, cover and simmer for 15 minutes.

Blend the kale and white bean mixture with rice and Parmesan until mostly smooth. Allow to cool and serve, or freeze in individual portions for later meals.

NOTE: You don't need large portions of the ingredients used. You can use leftover white beans in 4 Bean Vegetarian Chili (page 183), and leftover kale in Quick-Fix Tofu and Kale Stir-Fry (page 83). Use the remaining pumpkin to make another puree like my Pumpkin, Apple and Carrot Puree (page 131).

MUNCHKIN'S FRIED RICE

MAKES ¾ CUP (120 G)

This is a wonderful lunch or dinner for when you really don't have anything prepared and don't have much in your refrigerator but want to give your kid something healthy. It is also a great way of adding vegetables to your little one's meals since the peas and carrots are easily stored in the freezer.

For early finger foods, my son actually went through a stage where he loved anything round (including peas). Instead of picking around them, he would select them first. Hopefully your child enjoys that stage as well! Regardless, this is a tasty way of coaxing in those extra servings of veggies.

---

1 tbsp (15 ml) olive oil

½ cup (81 g) cooked jasmine rice (day old is great)

¼ cup (35 g) frozen peas and carrots

1 tbsp (15 ml) chicken stock

1 egg

1 tsp low-sodium soy sauce

In a medium-size sauté pan over medium-high heat, add the oil and heat for 1 minute. Add the rice, vegetables and stock, and cook, stirring frequently, for 2 minutes.

In a small bowl, whisk your egg. Add your egg to the rice mixture and stir until it coats the rice and is cooked through, 1 to 2 minutes. Add the soy sauce and stir until combined, 1 to 2 minutes. Serve once cooled.

NOTE: You can alternate the vegetables you add, substituting small broccoli florets, cut green beans, corn, asparagus or butternut squash. Just ensure everything is cooked until soft and offered in bite-size pieces that are easily chewable.

RINKLES' RISOTTO

MAKES 3½ CUPS (563 G)

There is no sensible reason for my son's nickname Rinkles, but there are plenty of reasons to enjoy this risotto. It is creamy, great for introducing textures and can be enjoyed by parents and youngsters alike. Best yet is that this version does not require constant stirring.

This is also a great dish for mixing up the vegetables you serve. My two favorite ways to serve this are with spring peas or with roasted diced butternut squash.

1 tbsp (14 g) butter

2 tbsp (19 g) finely chopped sweet onion

1 cup (211 g) arborio rice

3½ cups (828 ml) chicken stock, divided

½ cup (90 g) grated Parmesan cheese

½ cup (67 g) frozen sweet peas

In a medium-size stockpot over medium heat, add butter and warm until melted. Add the onions, and cook until they're softened, about 2 to 4 minutes. Add the rice and cook for 2 minutes, stirring several times. Add half the stock (1¾ cups [414 ml]) and stir once. Simmer for 10 to 12 minutes, until the liquid is absorbed. Stir in the remaining stock and simmer for 10 to 12 minutes, until most of the stock is absorbed. Stir in the Parmesan and peas, and allow to cool.

Serve slightly warm, always being mindful that infants have a greater sensitivity to heat, or at room temperature.

LEFTOVER RISOTTO

You can reheat leftover risotto by adding extra stock to it. The risotto will be softer than it was the first time, but it will still be tasty. For toddlers, you can mix it up by making fried risotto balls by breading and frying rounded balls of the leftover risotto. This makes a fun snack that is easy to handle for little ones who have moved on to finger foods.

NOTE: The nickname Rinkles is an evolution from Prinkles, which was a Scrabble joke turned into a two-year nicknaming streak that continued onto Rinkle-Stinkles, Bo Rinks, BR and Bunny Rinkles. Now I'm explaining to 3-year-olds why I call my son so many silly names.

SALMON AND SWEET POTATO PUREE

MAKES 2½ CUPS (592 ML)

Here is a complete meal in one puree. Salmon is a source of high-quality protein and omega-3 fatty acids. Omega-3s help keep the brain healthy and have been shown to help the symptoms of ADHD, depression and antisocial traits. These benefits, plus its delicious flavor, are all the reasons you need to make this puree.

1 tbsp (14 g) butter

¼ cup (22 g) sliced leeks

1 cup (133 g) diced sweet potato

¾ cup (96 g) finely diced carrots

1 cup (110 g) peeled, seeded and diced apple

1¼ cups (295 g) chicken stock

3 oz (85 g) salmon (you can increase this if you want a stronger salmon flavor)

Olive oil

Preheat your oven to 350°F (177°C).

In a medium-size stockpot, add the butter and leeks, and sauté over medium-high heat for 2 minutes. Next, add the sweet potato, carrots and apple, and stir to combine. Cover with the chicken stock and bring to a boil. Cover and reduce the heat to medium. Cook for 20 to 25 minutes, until the sweet potato and carrots fall apart when tested with a fork.

Meanwhile, line a small baking sheet with parchment paper and rub the salmon with olive oil. It is much easier to simply reserve a small portion of fish from when you cook salmon for dinner, but I wanted to do the full recipe here with a cook time for the salmon. Place the sheet in the oven, and cook the salmon for 8 to 12 minutes, until it flakes easily and is cooked through.

Once the salmon and sweet potato mixture have finished cooking, place them in a blender and pulse them together until you achieve a mostly smooth consistency with a bit of texture. How much texture you go for depends on your child. Cool, then serve or freeze in individual portions for later meals.

WINNER WINNER CHICKEN DINNER

MAKES 1¾ CUPS (368 G)

This is chicken soup for the baby's soul with tender chicken, sweet peas, carrots and stars. It tastes pretty much like a creamed chicken potpie. Dig in baby!

¼ cup (32 g) small diced carrots (it is important to dice them small for even boiling)

½ cup (118 ml) chicken stock

2 tbsp (18 g) frozen sweet peas

¼ cup (35 g) diced cooked chicken breast (oven-roasted chicken is great for tenderness)

1 cup (125 g) cooked star pasta (also called pastina), divided

In a small stockpot, combine the carrots with the stock, cover and bring to a boil. Reduce the heat to a low boil and cook for 15 minutes. Add the peas and cook for 5 minutes. The carrots should be tender and fall apart when tested by a fork. Then add the chicken and ½ cup (200 g) of star pasta. Puree in a blender or food processor until just smooth, then mix in the remaining stars.

Cool and serve or freeze in individual portions for later use.

LITTLE SHEPHERD'S PIE

FILLS 8 SMALL RAMEKINS

This is a complete baby meal that serves as a great transition from purees to chunkier meals. It is also perfect for adding herbs and spices into your baby's diet. Adding herbs and spices offers a baby new and interesting flavors to try without forcing you to season with salt, which a baby doesn't need.

3 cups (450 g) diced, peeled Idaho potatoes (3 small potatoes)

2 tbsp (28 g) butter, softened, plus more for topping

¼ cup (59 ml) whole milk

1 tbsp (15 ml) olive oil

1 lb (454 g) ground turkey

⅓ cup (78 ml) chicken stock

3 tbsp (44 ml) tomato sauce

Pinch of garlic powder

Pinch of onion powder

Pinch of thyme

¼ cup (34 g) frozen peas

¼ cup (40 g) frozen diced carrots

In a small stockpot, add the potatoes and cold water until the potatoes are just submerged. Boil until the potatoes are tender and fall apart when tested with a fork, 12 to 15 minutes. Strain the potatoes and then pass them through a potato ricer. You can always whip them with a blender or mash them with a fork, but whenever I want super creamy mashed potatoes, I always use a potato ricer. It is worth buying one just for this purpose.

In a small bowl, mix the riced potatoes with the butter and milk until blended. Set the potatoes aside as you cook your filling.

Add the olive oil to a medium-size sauté pan over medium-high heat. Brown your turkey for 5 to 7 minutes, until no pink remains. Add the chicken stock, tomato sauce, garlic powder, onion powder and thyme. At this point, you have the option of pureeing your meat, which will make it slightly more tender for your infant, or leaving it as is. If you puree the turkey, place it back in the pan and add the peas and carrots. Cook the filling for 2 to 3 minutes, until the veggies have softened. Test the carrots since they take longer.

To assemble, divide your filling evenly among 8 small ramekins, and top with mashed potatoes. Use a fork to create a pattern on top of each or simply to mash down. If desired, top the ramekins with a little melted butter. Broil for 2 minutes.

Be sure to allow to cool before serving. You can also freeze the remaining portions once fully cooled.

VARIATIONS

You can add even more vegetables to your baby's diet by substituting the pureed potato for sweet potato, butternut squash, carrot puree or any combination of the above.

NOTE: I know a pinch is not the most descriptive measurement, but when making such a small portion for a baby, ¼ teaspoon is simply too much. The amount you can pinch between your thumb and pointer finger is just about perfect.

MEAT TEXTURES TOTS LIKE

Some infants take immediately to the addition of meat to their diet, but others take longer. These are some options that are particularly tender and more likely to be accepted:

* Tender fish (salmon or whitefish like halibut or flounder are all great options).

* Meatballs are an excellent option for adding variety since you can mix up the filling, the seasoning or the meat you are using. Meatballs finished in sauce are the most tender since they soak up extra moisture while cooking.

* Meatloaf is another great choice much in line with meatballs. The recipe for Tender Turkey Meatloaf (page 194) has long been a favorite with my son.

* Pulled meats like chicken, brisket and pork are all great choices. Just be sure to mince the long strands into bites friendly for a young child.

* Roast chicken is delicious for early eaters. The skin works wonders at trapping moisture in the meat, so this may be some of the tenderest chicken you can offer your young child.

FINGER FOODS FOR TRAVEL

Chances are you will travel with your young child sometime during that first year. Once you've introduced solids, you may wonder what foods work for easy packing and minimal cleanup when in motion. Here's a handy list:

* Breakfast carbs such as waffles, pancakes, muffins and french toast all cut up easily into snackable bites. Make your own or choose premade options without added sugar.

* Diced fruit is a wonderfully healthy option for children who have moved on to finger foods. Apples, pears and berries are all handy choices.

* Steamed vegetables such as carrots, peas, corn and most frozen options already come in the perfect bite size. Sweet potato fries are also fun for chewing.

* Baby food pouches are convenient for travel. There are a great variety of organic options available. And for parents who want to make their own, there are pouches you can buy and easily refill with fresh, homemade purees.

- Crunchy snacks like cheddar crackers, puffs and Cheerios are all good options. The less processed you can find the better. Also look for options without heavy salt.

- For protein, rinsed canned beans, diced cooked chicken, cubed cheese, diced cooked tofu, string cheese, hummus, hard-boiled eggs and nut butters (after you've tested for allergies) all work well.

- Sandwich bites are excellent meals on the go. Great options are peanut butter and banana, avocado and cheese, cheese, hummus and tomato and cream cheese and smoked salmon.

- More substantial meals like mini quiches and pasta salads pack easily and make for fuller fare.

BABYPROOFING THE KITCHEN

As your baby begins crawling and pulling up, don't forget to babyproof your kitchen. Install an oven lock and knob covers for your oven. Cover outlets and move all breakables and cleaning supplies from lower shelves. Keep pan handles out of reach and cook on back burners.

I keep my plastic containers and kitchen towels in low cabinets so my son can pull them out and basically ransack at his pleasure. It took a little rearranging of my kitchen, but the result is a much safer setup and keeps him happy. I am used to cleanup, as most parents are by this time.

Baby walkers were also incredibly fun in our apartment. They keep infants at bay with their bumpers so that little ones can roam safely. And in a pinch, a baby gate to keep crawling children from the kitchen is another wonderful option.

FAMILY MEALS
(12 MONTHS AND UP)

As your child quickly progresses to eating the same foods as the rest of the family, it is important to have a good recipe bank to draw from. These are delicious meals to enjoy together. From the perfect Mommy and Me Green Smoothies (page 168) to the easiest, most succulent Friday Night Roast Rosemary Chicken (page 197), these are recipes you can keep coming back to. Your child will continue to develop, often testing your patience in the kitchen as you go through food battles, teething pains and other developmental hurdles. Just keep cooking, having a steady stream of options to entice your little one back to the table. You may also venture to have friends join you for dinner since it is often easier than meeting at a restaurant. Many of these meals make excellent options for effortless entertaining.

MOMMY AND ME GREEN SMOOTHIES

MAKES 5 CUPS (1 L)

Everyone needs a good recipe for a green drink. My goal was to find one that my husband and son would enjoy as much as I do. Smoothies are versatile. If you want to substitute baby kale for spinach, go ahead. If you prefer coconut water to almond milk, make the change. I just wanted to give my version, which I find utterly delicious and unbelievably healthy. This is our morning "go" juice.

2 cups (60 g) spinach, washed thoroughly

½ cup (52 g) roughly chopped English or Persian cucumber

1 cup (60 g) parsley

1 cup (165 g) diced yellow mango (1 yellow mango)

2 frozen bananas

2 cups (473 ml) almond milk, unsweetened

2 tbsp (23 g) peanut butter

In a strong blender, blend the spinach, cucumber, parsley, mango, bananas, almond milk and peanut butter together.

NOTE: Make 3 portions of the spinach, cucumber, parsley, mango, banana and peanut butter and freeze in 3 (1-gallon [4-L]) plastic resealable bags. This way you save yourself time in the morning. All you have to do is remove a bag from the freezer and blend it with almond milk. The frozen ingredients make a thicker smoothie, which travels well, especially in the hotter months. You also can thin the smoothie by adding extra almond milk until you reach your desired thickness.

SMALL BITES MINI QUICHE

MAKES 24

These mini quiches are wonderful because they are so easy to pop in your mouth as you run around trying to get out the door in the morning. If you have a toddler around, mini quiches are also great meals for them and a genius way to get them to eat vegetables.

Cooking spray

6 eggs

¾ cup (178 ml) half-and-half

Sea salt and freshly cracked pepper

¼ tsp nutmeg

½ cup (25 g) thinly sliced scallions (2 scallions)

¼ cup (37 g) finely diced red pepper

¼ cup (16 g) finely chopped cooked bacon (2 slices)

¾ cup (91 g) grated cheddar cheese

2 tbsp (23 g) grated Parmesan cheese

Preheat your oven to 375°F (190°C).

Spray two nonstick mini muffin tins with a heavy coating of cooking spray. In a medium bowl (it helps if you use one with a spout), whisk the eggs and half-and-half, and season with salt, pepper and nutmeg.

Divide your scallions, red pepper, bacon and cheddar evenly among your muffin tins. Pour your eggs on top of the filling, dividing the egg mixture evenly.

Bake for 10 minutes then top with the Parmesan and spray lightly with cooking spray once more. Broil on high for 2 to 4 minutes, checking every minute to prevent burning, until a toothpick inserted comes out clean and the tops are golden and bubbly.

These quiches will puff up like a soufflé and then deflate, but that is OK. They will taste good regardless of their height.

Allow to cool for 3 minutes, then remove with a spatula or fork, drawing it around the edges and popping out the quiches. It is OK if some egg mixture sticks to the tins; it doesn't have to be perfect.

If you are freezing them, pop the quiches in a resealable plastic bag once cool, and place them in the freezer. To reheat, set your oven to 350°F (190°C) and bake until warm through, about 10 minutes.

BAKED EGGS BRUNCH FOR THE SLEEP DEPRIVED

SERVES 4 TO 6

This is an amazing egg dish. To someone trying it for the first time it feels instantly exotic while still familiar. The tomato base is elevated with the toasted spices, all providing the perfect backdrop for oven-baked eggs. This is great to serve for brunch or while guests are in town, because once you set it down, everyone can serve themselves. I also love it as a weekend breakfast or a vegetarian dinner.

3 tbsp (45 ml) olive oil

1 cup (175 g) finely diced white onion

1 cup (149 g) finely diced red pepper

1 tbsp (9 g) chopped garlic (2 cloves)

½ tsp smoked paprika

½ tsp cumin

¼ tsp chili powder

Dash of cayenne

¼ tsp sea salt

1 (25.5-oz [709-ml]) jar tomato sauce or 3 cups (709 ml) homemade tomato sauce, plus 2 tsp (10 ml) tomato paste

5 oz (113 g) crumbled feta cheese

5 to 6 eggs depending on the size of your pan

Freshly cracked pepper

¼ cup (4 g) cilantro leaves, for garnish

Toasted pita, for dipping

Preheat your oven to 400°F (204°C).

In an oven-safe sauté pan or cast-iron pan, add the olive oil and onion, and cook on medium-high heat for 2 minutes. Add the red pepper and cook for 5 minutes, stirring from time to time until the onions are translucent and the peppers are soft. Add the garlic, paprika, cumin, chili powder, cayenne and salt. Stir to combine, then add the tomato sauce. Cook the tomato sauce until warmed, 2 to 3 minutes, then stir in the feta. Mix until the feta is evenly dispersed.

Using a large spoon, make several wells in the tomato sauce for your eggs. Slowly crack your eggs into the wells in the tomato sauce. Season the eggs with salt and pepper. Move the pan into the oven and bake for 10 to 20 minutes, until the eggs are just set. Check at 10 minutes, and watch from there until your eggs are the way you like them. Some people prefer their eggs a touch runny; I prefer them to have a soft yolk but firm white. Garnish with cilantro and serve with toasted pita.

MINESTRONE SOUP WITH DITALINI

SERVES 8 TO 10

I love making large pots of soup because it provides for countless family meals. Minestrone is one of my favorites because there are so many vegetables in it. Best yet, all the ingredients are moistened by the broth, making them the perfect texture for babies experimenting with small pieces of mushy food. This meal is also toddler friendly.

3 tbsp (45 ml) olive oil

1 cup (152 g) diced sweet onion

1 cup (128 g) diced carrots

1 cup (101 g) diced celery

1 cup (110 g) fresh green beans, cut into bite-size pieces

Sea salt and freshly cracked pepper

1 cup (265 g) diced zucchini

2 cloves garlic, minced or pressed

2 (32-oz [946-ml]) cartons of vegetable stock

1 (28-oz [794-g]) can diced tomatoes

1 (15.5-oz [439-g]) can red kidney beans, rinsed and drained

1 (15.5-oz [439-g]) can navy beans, rinsed and drained

½ cup (20 g) freshly chopped basil

3 cups (600 g) cooked ditalini pasta

Parmesan cheese, for serving

In a large stockpot, add the olive oil, onion, carrots, celery and green beans, and cook on high for 4 minutes, until softened. Stir to prevent scorching. Season with salt and pepper. Next, add the zucchini and cook for 4 minutes, until softened. Add the garlic and cook until fragrant, about 1 minute. Add the stock and diced tomatoes.

Bring the mixture to a boil, then reduce to a simmer and cook for 5 minutes. Add the kidney beans, navy beans and basil, and cook for 10 minutes to blend all the flavors. Add the pasta and cook for 1 minute. Remove from the heat and season once more to taste. Serve warm sprinkled with Parmesan.

NOTE: I love this soup even more the next day after the noodles have had a chance to soak in more of the stock and the vegetables have become even more tender.

CUT THE CARBS CHICKEN LETTUCE WRAPS

MAKES 15 LETTUCE WRAPS

These chicken lettuce wraps make a tasty appetizer or a healthy dinner for two. I make these for my husband and me after we've finally put our son down for the night. This meal, a nice stiff cocktail and suddenly it feels like we are on a date to one of our favorite NYC bars. A mom can dream at least . . .

The chicken is also incredibly toddler friendly when mixed with rice for your little one's lunch or dinner.

1 head Boston or butter lettuce

1 lb (454 g) boneless, skinless chicken thighs, diced into small pieces

1 tbsp (15 ml) sriracha, plus more for serving, optional (omit if you don't like heat)

1 tbsp (11 g) peanut butter

3 tbsp (45 ml) low-sodium soy sauce

1 tbsp (15 ml) hoisin sauce

1 tsp minced fresh ginger

2 cloves garlic, minced

1 (8-oz [227-g]) can sliced water chestnuts, drained and finely diced

1 tbsp (15 ml) sesame oil

¼ cup (12 g) sliced scallions (3 scallions)

¼ cup (40 g) chopped roasted peanuts

Line a baking sheet with paper towels, rinse the lettuce leaves and lay them on the sheet to dry.

In a medium bowl, add the chicken, sriracha, peanut butter, soy sauce, hoisin sauce, ginger, garlic and water chestnuts. Stir until the chicken is thoroughly coated and all the ingredients are mixed together.

In a large frying pan on high heat, add the sesame oil, and heat for 1 to 2 minutes. Add the chicken mixture, scraping down the sides of the bowl with a spatula to get all the sauce. Cook for 6 to 8 minutes, stirring as you go, until the chicken is slightly browned and cooked through. Remove the pan from the heat.

Lay out your lettuce leaves on plates or a tray. Spoon the chicken mixture onto the lettuce. Don't overfill; you want to be able to curl up the sides of the lettuce and pick them up easily. Top the chicken with scallions and peanuts. If you love sriracha (as my family does) drizzle the wraps with additional sauce and serve warm.

CHICKEN PITA SANDWICHES

MAKES 4 SANDWICHES

This is an amazingly flavorful meal that quickly became one of our family staples. I freeze flatbread so I have it whenever I want to make a pizza or one of these delicious and easy sandwiches. For my toddler, the chicken cut up and mixed with couscous is a winner. Extra diced cucumber and tomato make a simple finger food to complete the meal.

TURMERIC MARINATED CHICKEN

¼ cup (60 ml) olive oil

1 tsp turmeric

½ tsp hot smoked paprika

½ tsp garlic powder

½ tsp freshly cracked pepper

¼ tsp sea salt

½ tsp dried oregano

1 lb (454 g) chicken breast, cubed

YOGURT TAHINI DIP

1 cup (245 ml) full-fat yogurt

1 tbsp (15 ml) fresh lemon juice

¼ cup (59 ml) tahini

¼ tsp garlic powder

SANDWICHES

4 flatbreads

1 Persian or hothouse cucumber, thinly sliced

1 plum tomato, sliced

1 red onion, thinly sliced

Yogurt Tahini Dip

Sambal, optional

FOR THE TURMERIC MARINATED CHICKEN

Preheat your oven to broil.

In a large plastic resealable bag, add the oil, turmeric, paprika, garlic powder, pepper, salt, oregano and chicken. Seal the bag and shake until well combined. Marinate for at least 10 minutes or as long as overnight.

Broil your marinated chicken on high for about 5 minutes. Then switch your oven to 350°F (177°C) and toast your flatbread for about 3 minutes until warmed and a little toasty brown but not too crunchy.

FOR THE YOGURT TAHINI DIP

In a small bowl, mix the yogurt, lemon juice, tahini and garlic powder. Stir until well combined and refrigerate until ready to serve.

TO ASSEMBLE THE SANDWICHES

Top the flatbread with the chicken and dress it with cucumber, tomato and red onion. Finish by adding Yogurt Tahini Dip for a creamy flavor and sambal if you enjoy a little heat. Serve warm.

GOAT CHEESE AND ROASTED VEGGIE TART

SERVES 6 TO 8

This is a delightful vegetarian dinner that is perfect to make in advance. It is also a wonderful way to swaddle a lot of vegetables in creamy goat cheese to entice the little ones to eat their veggies. The pie crust is an extra step that I think is well worth it, but if you are trying to save time, you can always start with a frozen one from the store.

CRUST

1 cup (125 g) all-purpose flour

6 tbsp (85 g) cold butter (straight from the refrigerator)

2 to 3 tbsp (30 to 45 ml) cold water

TART

1 cup (175 g) seeded and diced red pepper (1 red pepper)

2 cups (76 g) beet greens, cleaned and chopped into ½-inch (1-cm) pieces

1 cup (152 g) diced red onion (1 small red onion)

1 cup (265 g) diced zucchini (1 small zucchini)

4 cups (328 g) diced eggplant (1 medium eggplant)

4 tbsp (60 ml) olive oil

Sea salt and freshly cracked pepper

1 cup (237 ml) heavy cream

2 eggs

½ tsp dried thyme

8 oz (227 g) herbed goat cheese, divided

TO MAKE THE CRUST

Mix the flour and butter in a large bowl until the butter resembles fine sand. Some lumps are OK and actually make for a very flaky crust. Alternately, you can use a standing mixer. Begin adding water 1 tablespoon (15 ml) at a time until you can easily roll your dough into a ball. I use the full 3 tablespoons (45 ml) because I like a moist dough.

Spread flour on a countertop and pat your rounded dough ball into a disc. Spread a little more flour on the dough (top and bottom) as well as on your rolling pin, and roll the dough into a circle 2 inches (5 cm) larger than your tart pan (I use a 10-inch [25.5-cm] pan but a standard 9-inch [23-cm] pie pan will work as well). You may need to add more flour as you continue to roll. Make sure to flip the disc so the bottom doesn't stick.

Gently fold the rolled dough into quarters and lay it into your pie pan. Unfold and press to the edges. Using a paring knife, cut off the dough hanging over the lip. Since this is an all-butter dough, it is very easy to patch any holes or fill in edges. Just press the dough together at the seams to fix. Crimp the edges to finish and line with a piece of parchment paper. Fill with pie weights or dry beans when ready to blind bake.

TO MAKE THE TART

Preheat your oven to 425°F (218°C).

Lay out 2 baking sheets and line one with parchment paper. On the parchment-lined sheet, lay out the red pepper, beet greens, onion, zucchini and eggplant, and toss with olive oil. Season with salt and pepper, and bake for 20 minutes. At the same time, lay your finished pie crust (filled with parchment and pie weights) on the second baking sheet and blind bake for 12 to 15 minutes, until the edges just begin to turn a tannish, golden brown (for a store-bought dough, allow it to defrost for 10 to 12 minutes, pinch any broken seams together before baking and blind bake for only 10 minutes). Once you take out your crust, toss the vegetables and return them to the oven until the eggplant has softened.

In a small mixing bowl (with a spout for easy pouring if you have one), mix your heavy cream with your eggs and thyme.

Remove and discard the parchment from your crust and save your pie weights. Top the crust with half the vegetables and half the goat cheese, crumbling as you go to spread it evenly, and then repeat with a second layer. Pour your heavy cream and egg evenly over the tart until all the surfaces are covered. Bake for 35 to 45 minutes, until a toothpick inserted comes out clean, with no egg clinging to it. You may have a bit of cooked goat cheese on the toothpick.

4 BEAN VEGETARIAN CHILI

SERVES 8 TO 10

This chili is a wonderful source of fiber and protein for the entire family. Aside from the onion, garlic and bell pepper, this dish is made from all pantry items. That means if you keep your pantry stocked, then you don't have to go to the store to get the makings of a great dinner. Saving a trip to the store is crucial, and even more so in the cold-weather months when this chili really hits the spot!

1 (15.5-oz [439-g]) can red kidney beans, divided

1 (15.5-oz [439-g]) can pink beans, divided

1 (15.5-oz [439-g]) can small white beans, divided

2 (14.5-oz [411-g]) cans black beans, divided

2 tbsp (30 ml) olive oil

2 cups (303 g) diced yellow onion (1 small yellow onion)

2 cups (350 g) diced green bell pepper (1 green bell pepper)

Salt and freshly cracked pepper

1 (14.5-oz [411-g]) can diced tomatoes

3 cloves garlic, minced

1 tbsp (10 g) cumin

¼ tsp cayenne, optional

1 cup (236 ml) green salsa (be sure you use a mild variety if you don't want it hot)

2½ cups (592 ml) vegetable stock, divided

GARNISH

Grated cheddar cheese

Sour cream

Pickled jalapeños, optional

Diced sweet onion, optional

Drain and rinse all the beans in a large colander. Heat the olive oil in a large stockpot or dutch oven. Add the onion and green bell pepper, and cook on medium-high heat, stirring several times until softened and the onions become translucent, 5 to 7 minutes. Reduce the heat to medium if the onions begin to scorch. Season with salt and pepper.

Add the tomatoes, garlic, cumin and cayenne if desired. Stir well and cook for about 1 minute. Add the green salsa, 1½ cups (360 ml) of vegetable stock and 1 cup (220 g) of mixed beans, and bring the mixture to a boil. Once it boils, reduce the heat to medium, and cook uncovered for 10 minutes.

Puree the mixture with an immersion blender (this creates a really nice thick base for the chili), then add the remaining beans and stock. Cook for 10 minutes more, until the beans are warm.

Serve topped with cheese, sour cream, jalapeños and onion if desired. Pair with 3 Cheese Chile Cornbread (page 184).

3 CHEESE CHILE CORNBREAD

SERVES 9

Chili and cornbread are a match made in heaven. The cheesy goodness of this cornbread
will make both parents and tots happy, and the green chiles add a lot of flavor without adding
too much heat, so you can serve your toddler as well.

1 cup (171 g) yellow cornmeal

1 cup (125 g) all-purpose flour

1 tbsp (11 g) baking powder

½ tsp salt

1 cup (121 g) grated sharp cheddar

1 cup (121 g) crumbled queso fresco

2 tbsp (23 g) grated Parmesan
cheese

1 cup (237 ml) buttermilk

¼ cup (57 g) butter, melted and
cooled

2 large eggs

1 (4-oz [113-g]) can diced green
chiles (4 oz), drained

3 tbsp (44 ml) honey

Preheat your oven to 375°F (190°C).

Grease an 8 × 8-inch (20.5 × 20.5-cm) baking pan.

In a large bowl, mix the cornmeal, flour, baking powder and salt together.
Add the cheeses.

In a small bowl, mix the buttermilk, butter, eggs, green chiles and honey
together. Slowly add your wet ingredients into your dry, and mix with a fork
until just combined. The batter will be slightly lumpy from all the cheese,
but that is OK.

Scrape down the sides of the bowl with a spatula and spoon the mixture
into the greased baking pan. Level the top, brush with butter or spray
with olive oil to brown the top, and bake for 25 to 33 minutes, until golden
brown around the edges and firm to the touch. Test with a skewer or
toothpick. Once it comes out clean, the cornbread is done.

Cool in the pan for 5 minutes, then slice into thirds lengthwise and thirds
widthwise (9 pieces), and serve warm.

CLOUDY DAY MEATBALLS

MAKES ABOUT 32 MEATBALLS

These are so ridiculously moist and tasty. They're great for serving to a baby who is on to finger foods and so adaptable for a family that doesn't like leftovers. I serve them over pasta, in a large skillet with French bread, as sliders on mini potato buns and as subs with extra sauce for dipping. They are as versatile as they are delicious.

1 (1.3-lb [590-g]) package ground turkey meat

1 egg

½ cup (54 g) dry bread crumbs

½ tsp freshly cracked pepper

¼ tsp sea salt

¼ cup (15 g) finely chopped fresh parsley

½ tsp garlic powder

¼ cup (60 ml) olive oil, for frying

3 cups (709 ml) tomato sauce

2 tbsp (23 g) grated Parmesan cheese

4 oz (56 g) fresh mozzarella cheese

French bread, optional for dipping

Potato buns, for meatball sliders

Submarine sandwich roll, for meatball sub sandwiches

Spaghetti, cooked according to package instructions, for spaghetti and meatballs

In a large bowl, mix the turkey, egg, bread crumbs, pepper, salt, parsley and garlic powder. Stir well until all the ingredients have mixed, then form into balls about the size of a ping-pong ball. Place the balls on a plate to the side.

Add olive oil to coat the bottom of a large frying pan. Warm the oil on medium-high heat for 1 to 2 minutes, then add your meatballs (if your pan is small, work in batches to avoid overcrowding). Cook the meatballs for about 2 minutes on the first side. I like to take the pan handle and shift it back and forth to roll the meatballs to cook other sides, but I still use a wooden spatula to turn any wayward meatballs to the undercooked sides. Do not despair when your meatballs are no longer perfectly round—they will still taste delicious! Your total cook time will be around 5 to 6 minutes per batch. Cook until the meatballs have two sides that are golden brown and are mostly browned on the edges. Remove to a clean plate when done with the first batch and repeat as needed.

Once all balls are cooked, return all the meatballs to the frying pan and cover with tomato sauce. Bring the sauce to a boil, then cook on medium heat for 20 minutes.

TO MAKE SKILLET MEATBALLS WITH FRENCH BREAD

Top with Parmesan and mozzarella, and cover with a lid until the cheese melts. Alternately, if you don't have a lid, cover with a baking sheet to trap the steam. Serve family style with fresh French bread for dipping.

(continued)

CLOUDY DAY MEATBALLS (CONT.)

TO MAKE MEATBALL SLIDERS
Serve meatballs on warmed potato buns. Cheese is optional but certainly welcome.

TO MAKE A MEATBALL SUB
Warm a sliced sub roll topped with slices of mozzarella cheese in the oven until the cheese melts, then top with meatballs and serve with extra warmed tomato sauce for dipping.

TO MAKE SPAGHETTI AND MEATBALLS
Boil your favorite noodles according to package instructions (spaghetti is one option but for little ones ditalini is nice because you don't have to chop it). I often cook the pasta an extra 2 minutes for my little one because he likes softer noodles. Dress your noodles with sauce, then cover with meatballs and a little Parmesan cheese or freshly grated mozzarella.

HEART-HEALTHY MUSSELS

SERVES 2

Mussels are not only incredibly tasty and affordable, but they are also packed full of health benefits for both adults and toddlers. Mussels are a great source of protein and selenium. Benefits of selenium include improved brain function, a strong immune system and, wait for it, improved fertility in both men and women! So when it's time to try for baby number 2, add some mussels to your diet.

My favorite way to enjoy mussels is in a garlic, wine and butter sauce. I always serve lots of extra bread for mopping up the delicious sauce as well as french fries on the side.

5 tbsp (71 g) salted butter, divided

1 large shallot, finely sliced

1 celery rib, finely sliced

2 cloves garlic, finely sliced

2½ cups (592 ml) dry white wine

½ pint (237 ml) heavy cream

2 lbs (907 g) mussels, cleaned

¾ cup (45 g) packed fresh parsley leaves, finely chopped

Sea salt

TO SERVE

Crusty bread

French fries

Aioli or mayonnaise

Belgian beer, optional

Heat 3 tablespoons (43 g) of butter in a large pot over medium-high heat. Add the shallot, celery and garlic, and cook until softened, about 7 minutes. Add the wine, cream and remaining butter, and bring to a boil. Add the mussels and parsley, season with salt and give it a good stir. Cover the pot and cook until the mussels open and are cooked through, about 10 to 15 minutes. Discard any mussels that do not open.

Serve with crusty bread, french fries, aioli and your favorite Belgian beer, if desired.

BUTTERNUT SQUASH AND CHICKPEA CURRY IN A HURRY

SERVES 6

This is a great vegan recipe. It is creamy and filling, and best of all it is a dinner that can be made in advance and heated as needed. Curries are great when friends are over because you already have your hands full and the last thing you want to do is cook. With this dish, you can just lay out a pot alongside a big bowl of jasmine rice and let everyone serve themselves.

For my son, I'll often mash the squash and chickpeas to make them smoother before stirring them into his rice. The creamy coconut broth is an easy favorite of his.

2 tbsp (30 ml) olive oil

¾ cup (114 g) chopped yellow onion (½ onion)

3 cloves garlic, minced

5 to 6 cups (700 to 840 g) butternut squash, peeled, seeded and diced to bite-size pieces (1 small butternut squash)

1 (13.5-oz [400-ml]) can full-fat coconut milk

2 tbsp (29 ml) Thai green curry paste (found in the Asian aisle in a supermarket)

1 cup (236 ml) vegetable stock

1 lime, juiced

1 (15.5-oz [439-g]) can chickpeas, drained and rinsed

1 (5- to 8-oz [141- to 227-g]) bag spinach, rinsed

½ cup (8 g) chopped cilantro leaves

Jasmine rice for serving

In a large stock pot with a lid or a Dutch oven, add the oil and onions, and cook for 3 minutes. Add the garlic, stir to combine then immediately add the squash, coconut milk, green curry paste, stock and lime juice. Bring to a boil, then cover and cook on medium heat for 30 to 35 minutes, until the squash is tender.

Mix in the chickpeas and spinach until they're coated in the sauce. Cover and cook for 5 to 7 minutes (organic chickpeas may take a few minutes longer to soften).

Toss in the cilantro when you're ready to serve, and serve alongside jasmine rice.

EVERYTHING-BUT-THE-KITCHEN-SINK FRITTATA

SERVES 8

Breakfast for dinner? Yes, please. Especially if you don't have time to shop for groceries, and you're trying to make use of what you have in your refrigerator.

I always have eggs. What I add to my frittatas depends on what else I have lying around. I love to add veggies, a mix of cheeses and sometimes sausage, salmon or bacon if I have them (not all together though). A frittata is versatile, toddler friendly and easily adaptable to many different flavors depending on the ingredients you have in your kitchen. Just keep your ratio of eggs to dairy the same to ensure the recipe turns out perfectly no matter how you flavor it.

3 tbsp (45 ml) olive oil, divided

8 oz (227 g) white button mushrooms, cleaned and sliced

Sea salt and freshly cracked pepper

1 yellow bell pepper, thinly sliced

3 cups (90 g) fresh spinach leaves

12 large eggs

½ cup (119 ml) half-and-half

¼ tsp nutmeg

1 cup (121 g) grated cheddar cheese, divided

Preheat your oven to 350°F (177°C).

Add 2 tablespoons (30 ml) of olive oil to a 12-inch (30.5-cm) oven-safe frying pan. Cast-iron pans work perfectly if you have one. Over medium-high heat, add the mushrooms in one layer. You may need to work in batches to prevent overcrowding. Cook for about 2 minutes per side. You are not cooking them until soft; you are frying them until they are a wonderful crispy golden brown. Transfer the finished mushrooms to a paper towel–lined plate and season with salt and pepper. Repeat until all the mushrooms are cooked.

Add the yellow pepper to the pan, and cook in the remaining oil for about 5 minutes, until softened. Add the spinach, and cook for 1 to 2 minutes, until wilted. Remove all the veggies to a separate bowl.

In a medium bowl, whisk the eggs with half-and-half. Season with salt and pepper and add the nutmeg. Add the remaining olive oil to the pan and swirl the pan until all sides are coated. Return all the veggies and mushrooms to the pan, and top with half of your grated cheese. Pour your egg mixture on top and finish with the remaining cheese.

Cook on medium-high heat on the stovetop until the eggs start to set, and then transfer to the oven. Bake in the oven for 12 to 15 minutes, until a knife inserted in the center comes out clean and reveals no runny egg.

Cool for 5 minutes, then slice and serve.

TENDER TURKEY MEATLOAF

SERVES 6

This is one of those recipes that is not overly impressive but will get you through many a weeknight and feed the whole family quite happily. Meatloaf has a soft texture for baby teeth and if your soon-to-be toddler is finicky on meaty textures it is a really good way to get them to enjoy it.

1 tbsp (15 ml) olive oil

½ cup (76 g) finely diced onion

½ cup (51 g) finely diced celery (1 rib celery)

2 large cloves garlic, minced

1 (1.3-lb [590-g]) package ground turkey meat

1 egg

¼ cup (11 g) fresh bread crumbs

¼ cup (27 g) dry bread crumbs

1 tsp Dijon mustard

½ tsp Worcestershire sauce

2 tsp (4 g) Italian seasoning or dried oregano

5 tbsp (73 ml) ketchup, divided

Sea salt and freshly cracked pepper

Preheat your oven to 350°F (177°C).

In a large pan, add the olive oil and cook the onion and celery on medium-high heat for 4 minutes. Stir to prevent the mixture from burning. Lower the heat to medium, add the garlic and cook for 1 minute.

In a large bowl, mix the turkey, egg, bread crumbs, mustard, Worcestershire sauce, Italian seasoning and 3 tablespoons (45 g) of ketchup. Season generously with salt and pepper.

Spoon the mixture into a loaf pan and level the top. Spoon the remaining ketchup on top in a thin layer and top with pepper, and bake for 1 hour.

Serve warm.

FRIDAY NIGHT ROAST ROSEMARY CHICKEN

SERVES 6

This is the ideal Friday night meal. A simple set-it-and-forget-it roast, and you have meals for the whole weekend. This chicken is perfect for using in baby purees or for serving to toddlers because the meat is so incredibly tender. Don't forget to save the bones to make the ultimate chicken broth for Mom's Cure-All Chicken Noodle Soup (page 19).

4 to 5 lbs (1.8 to 2 kg) whole chicken

3 to 4 tbsp (45 to 60 ml) olive oil

8 to 10 sprigs fresh rosemary

1 lemon

Sea salt and freshly cracked pepper

GRAVY

Pan drippings from roast chicken

1 tbsp (8 g) flour

¼ cup (59 ml) chicken stock

Sea salt and freshly cracked pepper

Preheat your oven to 450°F (232°C).

Pat the chicken dry with paper towels and remove any organs from the cavity. Dry the inner cavity as well. Place the chicken in a roasting dish and pour the olive oil on top. Rub the oil generously all over the chicken. Slide the rosemary under the skin covering the breasts on both sides. This should be easy to accomplish as your hands and the chicken will be covered in olive oil, so you should be able to slide several sprigs between the skin and the breast meat. Fill the cavity with the remaining rosemary. Slice the lemon in half and add both halves to the cavity as well.

Season the whole bird generously with salt and pepper, and roast for 45 minutes without opening the oven door. Test with a meat thermometer. Once the chicken is at 165°F (74°C), it is done. For a 5-pound (2-kg) bird, I roast for about 1 hour.

TO MAKE THE GRAVY

Take all the browned bits and liquid from the roasting pan and place in a small saucepan. Freeze it until the oil congeals, 10 to 15 minutes. Remove and discard the oil (the oil sits at the top and is yellow, not like the thick browned gel that is the liquid gold of gravy). Combine the browned gel with any drippings from the resting chicken. Heat until boiling.

Meanwhile, in a small container with a lid, mix the flour with the chicken stock. Cover tightly with the lid and shake vigorously until combined. Whisk into the drippings and cook until thickened. Remove from the heat and season to taste with salt and pepper.

SINFULLY SUCCULENT SKIRT STEAK AND MANGO SALAD

SERVES 4

My husband loves this "salad." I always love sneaking red meat into my salads because it instantly transforms the mundane into the seemingly sinful.

This is such a quick dish to make that it is easy to throw into your dinner rotation. The salad can be made in advance. Just save slicing the avocado and cooking the skirt steak until you're ready to serve. The noodles with avocado and mango are also great for toddler finger foods.

DRESSING

2 tbsp (30 ml) sesame oil

3 tbsp (45 ml) soy sauce

2 tbsp (30 ml) sweet chili sauce

1 tbsp (15 ml) sriracha (omit or use 1 tsp if you don't like heat)

1 lime, juiced

SALAD

6 cups (1.5 L) water

3 (3-oz [85-g]) packages ramen noodles

1 cup (165 g) diced mango

2½ cups (175 g) shredded cabbage (I like to do a mix of red and white)

½ cup (20 g) chopped fresh basil

½ cup (8 g) chopped fresh cilantro

½ cup (25 g) diced scallions (3 to 4 scallions depending on their size)

1 tbsp (15 ml) canola oil

1½ lbs (681 g) skirt steak

Sea salt and freshly cracked pepper

1 Hass avocado, diced

Sesame seeds for garnish

In a small bowl, combine the sesame oil, soy sauce, chili sauce, sriracha and lime juice.

Bring the water to a boil in a medium-size stockpot. Add the ramen and boil for 3 minutes. Strain and use kitchen shears to cut the ramen into shorter lengths for easy eating. I just snip several times in the colander to cut up the bigger clumps. Transfer the noodles to a large bowl and toss with the dressing. Add the mango, cabbage, basil, cilantro and scallions. Refrigerate until you're ready to cook your steak.

Bring your cooled ramen salad to the table to allow it to come to room temperature. In a large sauté pan, add the canola oil and heat for 1 minute. Meanwhile, season the steak generously with salt and pepper. Once the oil is hot, sear the steak for 2 to 3 minutes per side until it's medium rare, and set it on a board to cool for about 3 minutes before slicing.

As the steak is cooling, serve the salad on individual plates or one large platter. Top with diced avocado and sesame seeds. Then finish with the sliced seared steak. Serve warm.

IT'S OK NOT TO SHARE
JERK CHICKEN SANDWICHES

MAKES 4 SANDWICHES

This sandwich is pretty legendary as it almost ended my marriage. OK, a bit of an exaggeration on that one, but it definitely put a hiatus on the honeymoon period. On my actual honeymoon, my husband had scouted a cute café that was boasting these tasty sandwiches as he picked up our morning espresso. The rest of our day was planned around lunch, and when we finally sat down to eat, I said I wasn't really hungry and ordered a salad. Big mistake. To add insult to injury, I said I wanted "just a bite" of his sandwich but definitely took a wee bit more. As my husband describes it, all I left him with was a bite full of bread. Since that day, I've been trying to recreate this sandwich and atone.

For my toddler's meal, I like to serve the diced jerk chicken over rice with a side of diced mango.

JERK MARINADE
3 cloves garlic, minced

1 lime, juiced

1 tsp dried parsley

½ tsp dried thyme

½ tsp smoked paprika

½ tsp onion powder

¼ tsp ginger

¼ tsp nutmeg

¼ tsp cumin

¼ tsp red pepper flakes

½ tsp cinnamon

1 tsp brown sugar

1 tbsp (15 ml) olive oil

¼ tsp salt

1 tsp soy sauce

1 lb (454 g) thinly sliced chicken breast

RÉMOULADE SAUCE
1 tbsp (15 ml) lime juice

3 tbsp (44 ml) mayonnaise

1 tsp sriracha

½ tsp hot smoked paprika

MANGO RELISH
½ cup (83 g) finely chopped yellow mango

¼ cup (40 g) finely chopped tomato

1 tbsp (6 g) minced jalapeño, optional

1 tbsp (13 g) minced red onion

1 tsp chopped cilantro

1 tbsp (15 ml) lime juice

1 tsp olive oil

Sea salt

¼ tsp cumin

SANDWICH
2 tbsp (30 ml) vegetable oil

4 kaiser rolls

8 slices pepper jack cheese

4 leaves bibb lettuce

(continued)

Preheat your oven to 350°F (177°C).

TO MARINATE

In a gallon plastic resealable bag, combine the garlic, lime juice, parsley, thyme, smoked paprika, onion powder, ginger, nutmeg, cumin, red pepper flakes, cinnamon, brown sugar, olive oil, salt and soy sauce. Seal and shake to combine. Place the chicken breasts in the bag, seal and shake to distribute the marinade. Marinate for at least 10 minutes or overnight.

TO MAKE THE RÉMOULADE

In a small bowl, mix the lime juice, mayonnaise, sriracha and smoked paprika together. Refrigerate until ready to use.

TO MAKE THE MANGO RELISH

In a medium bowl, mix the mango, tomato, jalapeño, onion, cilantro, lime juice, olive oil, salt and cumin together. Cover with plastic wrap until ready to serve.

TO COOK THE CHICKEN

In a large sauté pan, add the vegetable oil and heat on medium-high heat, 1 to 2 minutes. Add the marinated chicken and cook for 2 to 4 minutes per side. The thinner it is sliced, the faster it will cook.

You want the pan preheated so you get a nice char on the surface of the chicken and the inside remains tender.

TO MAKE THE SANDWICHES

As the chicken is cooking, slice your rolls in half, place them on a baking sheet and dress all sides with the rémoulade. Top each half with a slice of cheese. Bake for about 4 minutes, until the buns have just toasted and the cheese has melted. Add the chicken to the bottom half of each roll, and top with lettuce and mango relish. Serve warm.

> **NOTE:** Do not be daunted by the list of ingredients; most are spices and pantry basics. If you don't have a lot of spices in your pantry, you can substitute a store-bought jerk rub for the jerk marinade to avoid buying multiple ingredients.

OUR FAVORITE FISH TACOS

MAKES ABOUT 11 TACOS (SERVES 2 TO 3)

No cookbook of mine would be complete without fish tacos. I often ask my husband what he wants for dinner, a futile question since the answer is always fish tacos. The beer batter is a must. The alcohol cooks off, but the crust is nice and crunchy and keeps the fish flaky and soft inside.

There are a lot of small steps to the recipe since we have truly perfected it over time. Don't be turned off by all the steps, they are quick and ensure that you will be enjoying the same amazing meal each time you prepare it.

I also give the pieces of fish to my toddler as fish sticks, and he loves them dipped in the avocado cream.

BEER BATTER
9 oz (273 ml) beer

1 cup (125 g) all-purpose flour

FISH RUB
¼ tsp garlic powder

¼ tsp smoked paprika

¼ tsp white pepper

¼ tsp coriander

AVOCADO CREAM
1 Hass avocado

½ cup (60 g) sour cream or Greek yogurt

1 lime, juiced

Sea salt to taste

FISH
2 flounder filets (about 1 lb [454 g] total) or other white fish, cut into 1 × 2-inch (2.5 × 5-cm) strips

¼ cup (60 ml) canola oil/vegetable oil, plus additional 1 to 2 tbsp (15 to 30 ml)

Sea salt and freshly cracked black pepper

Soft corn tortillas

FOR ASSEMBLING
1 cup (70 g) shredded cabbage

½ cup (8 g) cleaned cilantro leaves

1 tomato on the vine, diced

Line a baking sheet with paper towels.

TO MAKE THE BEER BATTER
In a medium bowl, mix your beer and flour until it is smooth and resembles pancake mix. Set aside.

TO MAKE THE FISH RUB
Combine your garlic powder, paprika, pepper and coriander in a 1-gallon (4-L) plastic resealable bag. Add your fish and shake until coated.

TO MAKE THE AVOCADO CREAM
In a medium bowl, mix the avocado, sour cream, lime juice and salt, mashing the avocado with the other ingredients until smooth. Set aside.

(continued)

TO FINISH YOUR FISH

Add ¼ cup (60 ml) of oil to your frying pan and bring to medium-high heat until sizzling, 1 to 2 minutes. Dip the seasoned fish into the batter, shaking off any excess before adding to your frying pan. Fry in batches until golden brown and flaky, 3 to 4 minutes per side. Remove the first batch to your paper towel–lined sheet and season with salt and pepper. Repeat with the second batch of fish, adding oil as needed. If the fish is turning dark too quickly, lower your temperature to medium, and cook until the fish flakes when tested with a fork.

TO TOAST TORTILLAS ON A GAS STOVE

Remove all the pans from the burners, and turn all your burners to medium-low heat. Lay a tortilla on each grate over the flames. Cook for about 30 seconds per side. You are looking for the tortillas to start to bubble slightly and just start to smoke (be sure to have your oven fan on for this step). You can use tongs or a fork if you are worried about getting burned.

TO ASSEMBLE

Top each tortilla with 2 to 3 pieces of fish, a sprinkle of cabbage, a sprig of cilantro and tomato. Drizzle with your avocado cream and serve warm.

NOTE: If you have leftover fish, you can freeze it on a parchment-lined baking sheet for 1 hour and then transfer to a plastic resealable bag. That way you can remove a portion when you want it, and reheat it in the oven at 350°F (177°C) until warmed through. Freezing helps preserve the crunchy exterior.

ONE-POT SHRIMP AND CREAMY PEANUT NOODLES WITH HIDDEN VEGGIES

SERVES 8

You'll love this meal for its hidden vegetables, richly seasoned noodles, and the fresh crunch of herbs and peanuts to finish. An added bonus of the one-pot meal is that cleanup is so easy and most of the work is in the chopping. Also, the vegetables seamlessly blend with the noodles in the peanut sauce making it a great way for toddlers to enjoy both (even if they don't realize it).

2 tbsp (30 ml) sesame oil

1 lb (454 g) uncooked shrimp (26 to 30 shrimp), cleaned

1 tsp smoked paprika

¼ tsp sea salt

5 cups (1 L) chicken stock

3 tbsp (45 ml) soy sauce

3 tbsp (33 g) peanut butter

1 tbsp (15 ml) hoisin sauce

1 tbsp (15 ml) sambal

3 cloves garlic, minced

1 (1-lb [454-g]) package linguine, broken in half

1 cup (265 g) zucchini, cut into matchsticks

1 red pepper, cut into matchsticks

1 cup (50 g) julienned carrots

1 cup (98 g) julienned fresh snow peas

1 lime, juiced plus additional wedges for garnish

1 cup (50 g) diced scallions

1 cup (16 g) cilantro leaves

1 cup (161 g) crushed roasted peanuts for garnish

In a large pot (make sure you have a lid), add the sesame oil and bring to medium-high heat. Season the shrimp with the smoked paprika and sea salt then cook for about 2 minutes, until the shrimp is just pink, and remove to a small plate. Add the chicken stock, soy sauce, peanut butter, hoisin, sambal and garlic to the pot. Cover and bring to a boil. Once boiling, stir in your linguine so that it is covered in sauce. Re-cover the pot and slightly lower the heat but keep the liquid at a low boil for 10 minutes.

After 10 minutes, add in the zucchini, red pepper, carrots and snow peas and cook for an additional 5 minutes, covered. Stir and taste a noodle. It should be nice and soft. Cook 1 to 2 more minutes if the noodles aren't tender. (Note: If you have added extra vegetables add a little extra chicken stock and allow slightly more time. Sometimes I add 1 cup [32 g] of bean sprouts.) You may have additional sauce after cooking but the noodles will continue to absorb it so this is a good thing.

Finish with the lime juice and stir. Turn off the heat and add the shrimp back in. Stir to combine and top with scallions, cilantro and crushed peanuts. Garnish with lime wedges and serve warm.

I CAN PRETEND IT'S DATE NIGHT GNOCCHI

SERVES 4

This recipe should not be on a dieter's list. It is sinfully creamy, cheesy and delicious, and should feel like the indulgence it is. I love having this on chilly nights because a bowl full of the soft, flavorful gnocchi is so very comforting and homey. It also makes a wonderful dinner for two. It can make you feel like you're eating at a small, beautifully laid table at an up-and-coming Italian spot without having to pay for a babysitter or travel farther than your own home. If you want to save time, you can purchase two 17.64-oz (500-g) packages of gnocchi instead of making them yourself.

For toddlers, I substitute a tomato sauce for the Gorgonzola cream sauce.

GNOCCHI

1 lb (456 g) ricotta cheese

1 cup (125 g) all-purpose flour

½ cup (90 g) grated Parmesan cheese

1 egg

½ tsp salt

SAUCE

1 pint (569 ml) heavy cream

3 oz (29 g) Gorgonzola, crumbled

4 tsp (15 g) grated Parmesan cheese

Salt and freshly cracked pepper

2 tbsp (8 g) chopped fresh parsley

½ cup (50 g) toasted walnut halves

TO MAKE THE GNOCCHI

In a large bowl, mix the ricotta, flour, Parmesan, egg and salt together, then refrigerate in plastic wrap for an hour.

Roll out the chilled dough with your hands into 1-inch (2.5-cm) coils. Slice into 1-inch (2.5-cm) pieces, and place them on a baking sheet lined with parchment paper. Repeat until all the gnocchi are rolled and cut. Freeze the gnocchi while you make your cream sauce (this helps them stay together during boiling).

TO MAKE THE SAUCE

Boil the cream for 40 minutes to reduce, stirring several times. Do not leave the room as the cream first comes to a boil or it may overflow the sides. Keep a loose watch to make sure the sauce bubbles but doesn't boil over. You may need to reduce your heat slightly during cooking.

As the cream sauce reduces, bring a large pot of salted water to a boil for your gnocchi.

To finish the cream sauce, remove from the heat and stir in the Gorgonzola and Parmesan. Season with salt and pepper and stir in the parsley. Leave the sauce on the stove but off the heat.

TO MAKE THE GNOCCHI

Add your gnocchi to the boiling water. They are done about 1 minute after they float to the top. Boil in batches to prevent sticking.

To finish, toss the gnocchi in the cream sauce and serve topped with toasted walnuts. If your Gorgonzola sauce is too thick, add a bit of the salted pasta water to thin it.

CREAMY CURRY CHICKEN PENNE

SERVES 6

This recipe is such comfort food: creamy pasta with a little kick from the curry and the perfect blend of flavors from the sundried tomatoes and broccoli. A cream sauce is a nice way to entice a toddler who is not too keen about broccoli to try it. Perfect for any weekday, here is a complete meal in a bowl.

1 lb (454 g) penne pasta

1 tbsp (15 ml) olive oil

1 lb (454 g) chicken breast, diced small

Sea salt and freshly cracked pepper

4 cups (624 g) frozen broccoli florets

1 cup (240 ml) chicken stock

½ cup (119 ml) half-and-half

1 tbsp plus 1 tsp (22 g) curry powder (yes that much, trust me)

1 cup (236 ml) Greek yogurt

1 cup (54 g) sundried tomatoes, cut into strips

½ cup (90 g) grated Parmesan cheese

Cook the penne according to package instructions. Reserve 1 cup (237 ml) of the salted boiling water.

In a large frying pan, add the olive oil and chicken, and cook on high heat for 4 to 5 minutes, until nicely browned and no pink remains. Season with salt and pepper and set aside on a large plate, making sure to preserve the juices from the pan. Simply pour any remaining juices onto the chicken as it rests.

Next, add the broccoli and ¼ cup (60 ml) of the reserved pasta water, and steam, covered, for about 3 minutes, until the broccoli is warm. Remove the broccoli to the plate with the chicken.

In the frying pan, add the chicken stock and half-and-half, and bring to a boil. Keep at a rolling boil for about 2 minutes, whisking as bubbles form and the mixture reduces. Add the curry powder. Whisk in the yogurt until creamy, and season with salt and pepper to taste.

Add the cooked penne into the sauce and mix. Then add the chicken, broccoli and sundried tomatoes, and mix until every morsel is coated in creamy sauce. Finish with the Parmesan, stir to blend and serve warm.

NOTE: You can refresh the cream sauce for leftovers with the salted water from the pasta, extra chicken stock or half-and-half.

IMPRESSIVELY EASY ROLLED HANGER STEAK WITH GOAT CHEESE AND SPINACH

SERVES 4 TO 6

This dish makes you look like such a rock star when you serve it, but it takes minimal time to make. The hardest part is probably tying up the rolled steak with twine, but it's something we all imagine doing to our kids when they act up, so this step gives us some much-needed therapeutic release.

This is another great "date night in" recipe for parents. For toddlers, I mince the steak for easier chewing and serve it mixed with rice. Then I puree the spinach and goat cheese then serve it on the side as a creamed spinach.

3 tbsp (45 ml) olive oil, divided

1 (10-oz [283-g]) bag fresh baby spinach leaves, rinsed

½ cup (75 g) minced white onion

1 lb (454 g) hanger steak, trimmed and pounded thin

Salt and freshly cracked pepper

3½ oz (99 g) herbed goat cheese

¼ cup (14 g) sundried tomatoes, chopped

3 cloves garlic, minced

Preheat your oven to 425°F (218°C).

In a large frying pan, add 1 tablespoon (15 ml) of olive oil, and cook your spinach until wilted. Stir as you go. It should take only 1 to 2 minutes. Remove the spinach and cool in a small bowl.

Add 1 tablespoon (15 ml) of olive oil, and cook your onion for 2 to 3 minutes, until translucent. Cook on medium-low heat so the onion doesn't scorch. Set aside in a medium bowl.

Line a baking sheet with aluminum foil and lay out your hanger steak. Season generously with salt and pepper.

When your spinach is cool enough to handle, wring out all the liquid. Really wring it hard—you don't want any of it in the dish. Combine the spinach with the onion and add the goat cheese, sundried tomato and garlic. Mix and season with pepper.

Spread your spinach mixture evenly over your hanger steak, pressing it out to all sides. Roll your hanger steak tightly, and tie it with butcher's twine to keep it together. Add your remaining olive oil to the pan and heat to high. Sear the rolled hanger steak on all sides, about 1 minute per side, turning with tongs as you go. Season the rolled hanger steak on all sides once again with salt and pepper, and place on the foil-lined baking sheet.

Bake in the oven for 30 minutes, and then allow to cool for 10 minutes. Once cool, cut off the butcher's twine and slice into 6 pieces. Serve each one face up so guests can see the rolled layers and be awed by your prowess in the kitchen. Feel very good about yourself, and then dig in!

BIXBY'S LIQUID FIRE BRISKET

SERVES 8 TO 10

My friend Tara has one the best brisket recipes I have ever tasted, and one of her secrets is liquid smoke. I really had no idea what it was before I saw it in her recipe. It is basically the goodness of a BBQ pit captured in a small jar. I sent my husband to the store to find it for me but later found out he was asking for liquid fire. I have to laugh because he always has a way of making things seem cooler.

This is an adaptation of Tara's recipe, named for her awesome son Bixby, that makes super tender, pull-apart brisket adored by adults and toddlers alike.

---

6 oz (164 ml) ketchup

¼ cup (60 ml) liquid smoke, usually found in the same aisle as BBQ sauce

1½ tsp (8 g) garlic salt

1½ tsp (4 g) onion powder

½ tsp cayenne

½ tsp freshly cracked pepper

½ tsp dry mustard

1½ tsp (8 ml) Worcestershire sauce

4 to 5 lbs (1.8 to 2 kg) brisket, fat trimmed

Preheat your oven to 375°F (190°C).

Fill a 9 × 12-inch (23 × 30.5-cm) casserole dish or a Dutch oven with 1 inch (2.5 cm) of water. You can use whatever dish you normally bake in as long as the sides are at least 2 inches (5 cm) high.

In a medium bowl, mix the ketchup, liquid smoke, garlic salt, onion powder, cayenne, pepper, dry mustard and Worcestershire sauce together.

Lay your brisket fat side up in your prepared baking dish, and pour sauce over it until the brisket is coated. Cover your baking dish with a lid if it has one or aluminum foil, and bake 1 hour per pound (454 g). Your brisket will be done when it is tender enough to fall apart easily when tested with a fork. Allow to cool, then shred the brisket with a fork. Discard any residual fatty bits.

Place the shredded brisket in a serving dish, then take the remaining sauce from your baking dish and place in a small bowl to freeze for about 15 minutes. Remove the top layer of fat with a spoon and discard. Then put the remaining sauce in a medium sauce pan over medium-high heat and boil until the liquid reduces by half, 10 to 15 minutes. Pour the sauce over the brisket and stir until every piece is coated. Serve warm.

NOTE: Don't let the long bake time deter you. This is a very easy recipe that freezes well and can be served in so many recipes, including Brisket Tacos (page 218) and Brisket Sliders with Carrot Cilantro Slaw (page 217). I make it the night before I plan on serving due to the long bake time, and double the recipe for holidays because it is so popular with a crowd.

BRISKET SLIDERS WITH CARROT CILANTRO SLAW

SERVES 4

These sliders make for an insanely tasty meal. The carrot slaw adds great fiber and is a fun switch from traditional coleslaw as a topping. The brisket is a tender meat for babies once minced very fine, and for toddlers, it can be cut into smaller strands for mini sandwiches with carrot slaw on the side. When making the carrot slaw for toddlers, I pull out a portion of the carrots and dress them separately (uncooked scallions and cilantro are really strong tastes for toddlers).

2 lbs (907 g) cooked brisket

4 potato rolls or brioche buns for serving

CARROT CILANTRO SLAW

½ tsp honey

2 tbsp (30 ml) olive oil

¼ tsp cumin

1 clove garlic, minced

¼ tsp salt

2 cups (220 g) grated carrot

1 cup (16 g) cilantro leaves

⅓ cup (34 g) sliced scallions (about 2 scallions)

In a medium stockpot, reheat the brisket on medium-low until warmed through.

In a small bowl, whisk the honey, olive oil, cumin, garlic and salt as a dressing for your carrot slaw. In a medium bowl, mix the carrot, cilantro and scallions. Dress the carrot mixture to taste with the dressing.

To assemble the sliders, divide the cooked brisket between 4 buns, and top with the Carrot Cilantro Slaw, or serve it as a side.

BRISKET TACOS

SERVES 4 TO 6

Brisket makes killer tacos. Once the brisket is already cooked, this recipe flies together, giving you dinner at the snap of a finger. For toddlers, you can make an easy brisket bowl by adding chopped brisket to rice and topping it with diced tomato, diced avocado and cheese.

---

2 to 3 lbs (907 g to 1.4 kg) cooked brisket

Soft corn tortillas

TOPPINGS

2 tomatoes on the vine, sliced

¼ red onion, thinly sliced

½ cup (8 g) cilantro leaves

1 Hass avocado, diced

1 jalapeño, thinly sliced

¾ cup (75 g) crumbled cotija cheese

In a medium stockpot, reheat the brisket on medium-low until warmed through. Then toast your tortillas.

TO TOAST TORTILLAS ON A GAS STOVE

Remove all pans from the burners and turn all your burners to medium-low heat. Lay a tortilla on each grate over the flames. Cook for about 30 seconds per side. You are looking for the tortillas to start to bubble slightly and just start to smoke (be sure to have your oven fan on for this step). You can use tongs or a fork if you are worried about getting burned.

To assemble, top each tortilla with a large forkful of brisket, and dress it with your tomatoes, red onion, cilantro, avocado, jalapeño and crumbled cotija cheese. Serve immediately.

ACKNOWLEDGMENTS

To Josh, the love of my life, without whom none of this would have been possible; Master Jack, who makes it all worthwhile; and sweet Lila, who makes our family complete.

It takes a village, and mine is ever expanding. To Lindsey, who introduced me to my husband at a bar one lucky night, and to my Sex in the City gang!

To my parents, who made my childhood completely awesome and taught me my love of the kitchen. Mom, so much of this cookbook we did together.

To the infamous Lars and the Little General, I'm so lucky to call you family. June, thank you for keeping this project marching to fruition. This book was a family effort and much of it sprang to life on visits from grandparents.

To the original Bubby, a.k.a. Uncle O and Uncle J, a.k.a. Dr. Satler. To my grandma, who taught me how to bake my first pie, and to Mj and Bill and Aunt Mary and Unc Unc. To all of Jack's aunties, Ande, Brace, Katie, Lindsey, Rachel, Tara and Queen Elizabeth, for their support with this book and friendship over the years.

Thank you to the fabulous Astoria gang of rowdy toddlers who found each other, and, of course, their moms and dads, who are often my salvation. Thank you to the wonderful moms and infants who I got to photograph for this book: Stephanie, Magan, Heather and Séamus, Zoe, Lilou, Landon, Gus, Eddie and Lily. To the Radoncics for letting me hoard wood boards and photograph in their backyard and for always treating us like family. To the employees at Lumber Liquidators, Inc., for giving me wood to photograph, and for not laughing when I showed up in my mom clothes with stroller and baby to pick it up.

To Val for proving time and again through your generosity that women can make the best bosses and mentors. To Harold for your early direction with this book. To the infamous Uncle Pomp. To Laurie, who is the greatest mentor and friend. To John Blondel for starting me on this culinary journey. To Dr. Tang and the nurses who delivered our two healthy, beautiful babies, thank you guys for being so incredibly good at what you do. To Dr. Piechev for being a pediatrician my son enjoys visiting even on vaccination days! To Michelle who is a true friend with crazy professional skills who has answered so many of our nervous parent texts. Importantly, thanks to Allison for jumping onboard and adding her insane expertise to make this book a reality.

Thank you to Marissa, Meg, Ruth, Will and everyone at Page Street Publishing.

ABOUT THE AUTHORS

AURORA SATLER, AUTHOR

For five years, Aurora worked as the creative director of Many Kitchens, an e-commerce site devoted to promoting the best small-batch artisanal food throughout the nation. She styled the cookbook *Recipes from Many Kitchens*. Previously, Aurora owned her own New York City catering company and wrote for *Chile Pepper* magazine. She is a graduate of NYU and the Institute of Culinary Education. You may have seen her or just her hands in numerous culinary tutorials, and her work as a food stylist is dispersed throughout Web, print and video. She's a proud mother, an urban gardener and a photographer who is happiest capturing delicious food and delightful smiles. She lives in New York City with her husband and two small children.

ALLISON CHILDRESS, NUTRITIONIST

Allison Childress PhD, RDN, CSSD, LD, is an assistant professor at Texas Tech University and chief clinical dietitian at the Nutrition and Metabolic Health Institute. She is a licensed dietitian in Texas and New Mexico and maintains a consulting practice as well. Allison is board certified in sports dietetics as well as a certified personal trainer. She has experience as a clinical and consultant registered dietitian specializing in cardiac, women's health, bariatric, pediatric and geriatric nutrition as well as weight management. She currently resides in Lubbock, Texas, with her husband, John; her three children, Bo, Taylor and Landrie; and her beloved goldendoodle, Oakley.

INDEX

apples
   Apple, Carrot and Ginger Muffins, 99
   Apple, Sweet Potato and Corn Puree, 127
   Grandma's Effortless Applesauce, 96
   Pumpkin, Apple and Carrot Puree, 131
   Salmon and Sweet Potato Puree, 159
avocados
   Baby Guacamole, 124
   Black Bean and Quinoa Burgers, 59
   Brisket Tacos, 218
   Freezer-Friendly Chicken Chile Enchiladas, 55
   Gotta Rehydrate Cucumber Tomato Salad, 76
   Mama's Guacamole, 74
   Our Favorite Fish Tacos, 203–205
   Sinfully Succulent Skirt Steak and Mango
     Salad, 198
   So-Easy-It's-Sinful Rice and Bean Bowls, 84

bacon, for Small Bites Mini Quiche, 171
bananas
   Banana Rice Pudding, 151
   Bun in the Oven Banana Zucchini Bread, 12
   Mommy and Me Green Smoothies, 168
   Very Berry Puree, 132
beef brisket
   Bixby's Liquid Fire Brisket, 214
   Brisket Sliders with Carrot Cilantro Slaw, 217
   Brisket Tacos, 218
beef, hanger steak, for Impressively Easy Rolled
     Hanger Steak with Goat Cheese and
     Spinach, 213
beef, skirt steak, for Sinfully Succulent Skirt Steak
     and Mango Salad, 198
black beans
   4 Bean Vegetarian Chili, 183
   Black Bean and Quinoa Burgers, 59
   So-Easy-It's-Sinful Rice and Bean Bowls, 84
   Southwest Sweet Potato Cakes and Black Bean
     Salsa Fresca, 115
blueberries
   Blueberry Buttermilk Pancakes, 48
   Very Berry Puree, 132
breastfeeding
   alcohol and, 88
   nutrition and, 88
   resources, 89
brisket
   Bixby's Liquid Fire Brisket, 214
   Brisket Sliders with Carrot Cilantro Slaw, 217
   Brisket Tacos, 218
broccoli
   Creamy Curry Chicken Penne, 210
   Grab-and-Go Green Pasta Salad, 80
   Munchkin's Fried Rice, 155
   Soba Noodle and Broccoli Rabe Buddha Bowl, 87

cabbage
   Our Favorite Fish Tacos, 203–205
   Sinfully Succulent Skirt Steak and Mango Salad,
     198
carrots
   Apple, Carrot and Ginger Muffins, 99
   Brisket Sliders with Carrot Cilantro Slaw, 217
   Carrot Cumin Soup, 111
   Carrot Puree, 108

Creamed Corn and Chicken Casserole, 140
Goddess Dressing with Crudités, 70
Little Shepherd's Pie, 163
Minestrone Soup with Ditalini, 175
Mom's Cure-All Chicken Noodle Soup, 19
Munchkin's Fried Rice, 155
One-Pot Shrimp and Creamy Peanut Noodles with
   Hidden Veggies, 206
Pumpkin, Apple and Carrot Puree, 131
Salmon and Sweet Potato Puree, 159
The Ultimate Chicken Broth, 19
celery
   Don't-Need-No-Deli-Meat Chicken Salad
     Sandwich, 20
   Heart-Healthy Mussels, 189
   Minestrone Soup with Ditalini, 175
   Mom's Cure-All Chicken Noodle Soup, 19
   Tender Turkey Meatloaf, 194
cheddar cheese
   3 Cheese Chile Cornbread, 184
   4 Bean Vegetarian Chili, 183
   Black Bean and Quinoa Burgers, 59
   Butternut Squash Mac 'n' Cheese, 107
   Everything-but-the-Kitchen-Sink Frittata, 193
   Freezer-Friendly Chicken Chile Enchiladas, 55
   Small Bites Mini Quiche, 171
   So-Easy-It's-Sinful Rice and Bean Bowls, 84
   Southwest Sweet Potato Cakes and Black Bean
     Salsa Fresca, 115
chicken breasts
   Baby's Eviction Notice Pineapple Teriyaki Chicken
     Stir-Fry, 64
   Chicken Pita Sandwiches, 179
   Creamed Corn and Chicken Casserole, 140
   Creamy Curry Chicken Penne, 210
   Don't-Need-No-Deli-Meat Chicken Salad
     Sandwich, 20

   I ♥ Peanut Butter Chicken Skewers, 24
   It's OK Not to Share Jerk Chicken Sandwiches,
     201–202
   Mom's Cure-All Chicken Noodle Soup, 19
   Winner Winner Chicken Dinner, 160
chicken, diced
   Freezer-Friendly Chicken Chile Enchiladas, 55
   Winner Winner Chicken Dinner, 160
chicken sausage, for Mom-to-Be Sausage and
     Veggie Ziti, 56
chicken thighs, for Cut the Carbs Chicken Lettuce
     Wraps, 176
chicken, whole
   Friday Night Roast Rosemary Chicken, 197
   Mom's Cure-All Chicken Noodle Soup, 19
   The Ultimate Chicken Broth, 19
chickpeas, for Butternut Squash and Chickpea
     Curry in a Hurry, 190
corn
   3 Cheese Chile Cornbread, 184
   Apple, Sweet Potato and Corn Puree, 127
   Black Bean and Quinoa Burgers, 59
   Creamed Corn and Chicken Casserole, 140
   Munchkin's Fried Rice, 155
cotija cheese, for Brisket Tacos, 218
cranberries
   Baby Shower "Sangria," 36

Don't-Need-No-Deli-Meat Chicken Salad
   Sandwich, 20
cream cheese, for Calcium-Rich Whipped Feta Dip,
   73
cucumbers
   Chicken Pita Sandwiches, 179
   Goddess Dressing with Crudités, 70
   Gotta Rehydrate Cucumber Tomato Salad, 76
   Mommy and Me Green Smoothies, 168
   Prego Picnic Chili Lime Fruit Cones, 31
curry
   Butternut Squash and Chickpea Curry in a Hurry,
     190
   Creamy Curry Chicken Penne, 210

eggplant
   40-Weeks-and-Counting Spicy Eggplant
     Parmesan, 63
   Goat Cheese and Roasted Veggie Tart, 180–181
eggs
   3 Cheese Chile Cornbread, 184
   40-Weeks-and-Counting Spicy Eggplant
     Parmesan, 63
   Apple, Carrot and Ginger Muffins, 99
   Baked Eggs Brunch for the Sleep Deprived, 172
   Black Bean and Quinoa Burgers, 59
   Blueberry Buttermilk Pancakes, 48
   Bun in the Oven Banana Zucchini Bread, 12
   Cloudy Day Meatballs, 185
   Everything-but-the-Kitchen-Sink Frittata, 193
   Fork-Free Turkey and Mushroom Hand Pies, 60
   Goat Cheese and Roasted Veggie Tart, 180–181
   I Can Pretend It's Date Night Gnocchi, 209
   Munchkin's Fried Rice, 155
   Small Bites Mini Quiche, 171
   Tender Turkey Meatloaf, 194

feta cheese
   Baked Eggs Brunch for the Sleep Deprived, 172
   Calcium-Rich Whipped Feta Dip, 73
   Orzo and Sundried Tomato Salad, 79
first foods
   equipment for solid foods, 94–95
   no-cook foods, 95
   portion sizes, 121
   solid foods, 93, 94–95
   timeline, 92
   tips for, 121
fish and seafood
   avoiding, 38
   Heart-Healthy Mussels, 189
   One-Pot Shrimp and Creamy Peanut Noodles with
     Hidden Veggies, 206
   Our Favorite Fish Tacos, 203–205
   Salmon and Sweet Potato Puree, 159
fruit purees
   Apple, Sweet Potato and Corn Puree, 127
   Mango Puree, 116
   Mango Sorbet, 119
   Pear and Oat Smoothie, 103
   Pear, Kiwi and Spinach Puree, 128
   Pear Puree, 100
   Pumpkin, Apple and Carrot Puree, 131
   Very Berry Coconut Popsicles, 135
   Very Berry Oatmeal Breakfast, 148
   Very Berry Puree, 132

garlic
  4 Bean Vegetarian Chili, 183
  Baked Eggs Brunch for the Sleep Deprived, 172
  Black Bean and Quinoa Burgers, 59
  Brisket Sliders with Carrot Cilantro Slaw, 217
  Butternut Squash and Chickpea Curry in a
    Hurry, 190
  Carrot Cumin Soup, 111
  Creamy Lemon Comfort Rice, 16
  Cut the Carbs Chicken Lettuce Wraps, 176
  Fork-Free Turkey and Mushroom Hand Pies, 60
  Freeze-by-the-Batch Tomato Sauce, 51
  Goddess Dressing with Crudités, 70
  Heart-Healthy Mussels, 189
  I ♥ Peanut Butter Chicken Skewers, 24
  Impressively Easy Rolled Hanger Steak with Goat
    Cheese and Spinach, 213
  It's OK Not to Share Jerk Chicken Sandwiches,
    201–202
  Minestrone Soup with Ditalini, 175
  Mom's Cure-All Chicken Noodle Soup, 19
  One-Pot Shrimp and Creamy Peanut Noodles with
    Hidden Veggies, 206
  Soba Noodle and Broccoli Rabe Buddha Bowl, 87
  Southwest Sweet Potato Cakes and Black Bean
    Salsa Fresca, 115
  Tender Turkey Meatloaf, 194
  Truffle Parmesan Crack Fries, 23
  The Ultimate Chicken Broth, 19
ginger
  Apple, Carrot and Ginger Muffins, 99
  Cut the Carbs Chicken Lettuce Wraps, 176
  Happy Tummy Gingery Lemonade, 15
  I ♥ Peanut Butter Chicken Skewers, 24
  Pear and Oat Smoothie, 103
  Pear Puree, 100
goat cheese
  Full-Term Twice-Baked Potatoes, 28
  Goat Cheese and Roasted Veggie Tart, 180–181
  Impressively Easy Rolled Hanger Steak with Goat
    Cheese and Spinach, 213
Gorgonzola cheese, for I Can Pretend It's Date Night
  Gnocchi, 209
green beans
  Grab-and-Go Green Pasta Salad, 80
  Minestrone Soup with Ditalini, 175
greens, for Goat Cheese and Roasted Veggie Tart,
  180–181
Gruyere cheese, for Butternut Squash Mac 'n'
  Cheese, 107

jalapeño peppers
  4 Bean Vegetarian Chili, 183
  Baby Needs Pizza Home-Baked Remedy, 27
  Brisket Tacos, 218
  Calcium-Rich Whipped Feta Dip, 73
  Freezer-Friendly Chicken Chile Enchiladas, 55
  Home-Style Salsa, 75
  It's OK Not to Share Jerk Chicken Sandwiches,
    201–202
  Jalapeño Simple Syrup, 32
  Mama's Guacamole, 74
  So-Easy-It's-Sinful Rice and Bean Bowls, 84
  Southwest Sweet Potato Cakes and Black Bean
    Salsa Fresca, 115
  Tropical Tummy Mango Faux-'Jito, 32
kale
  Quick-Fix Tofu and Kale Stir-Fry, 83
  White Bean, Pumpkin and Kale Puree, 152

kidney beans
  4 Bean Vegetarian Chili, 183
  Minestrone Soup with Ditalini, 175
kiwi, for Pear, Kiwi and Spinach Puree, 128

leeks
  Pea, Potato and Leek Puree, 136
  Pea, Potato and Leek Soup, 139
  Salmon and Sweet Potato Puree, 159

mangoes
  It's OK Not to Share Jerk Chicken Sandwiches,
    201–202
  Jalapeño Simple Syrup, 32
  Mango Puree, 116
  Mango Sorbet, 119
  Mommy and Me Green Smoothies, 168
  Prego Picnic Chili Lime Fruit Cones, 31
  Sinfully Succulent Skirt Steak and Mango Salad,
    198
  Tropical Tummy Mango Faux-'Jito
milk, cow's milk
  Butternut Squash Mac 'n' Cheese, 107
  Full-Term Twice-Baked Potatoes, 28
  Little Shepherd's Pie, 163
mozzarella cheese
  40-Weeks-and-Counting Spicy Eggplant Parme-
    san, 63
  Baby Needs Pizza Home-Baked Remedy, 27
  Cloudy Day Meatballs, 185–186
  Fork-Free Turkey and Mushroom Hand Pies, 60
  Mom-to-Be Sausage and Veggie Ziti, 56
mushrooms
  Everything-but-the-Kitchen-Sink Frittata, 193
  Fork-Free Turkey and Mushroom Hand Pies, 60
mussels, for Heart-Healthy Mussels, 189

navy beans, for Minestrone Soup with Ditalini, 175

oats
  Bun in the Oven Banana Zucchini Bread, 12
  Home-Baked Granola, 44
  Pear and Oat Smoothie, 103
  Very Berry Oatmeal Breakfast, 148
onions, red
  Black Bean and Quinoa Burgers, 59
  Brisket Tacos, 218
  Chicken Pita Sandwiches, 179
  Goat Cheese and Roasted Veggie Tart, 180–181
  Gotta Rehydrate Cucumber Tomato Salad, 76
  Home-Style Salsa, 75
  It's OK Not to Share Jerk Chicken Sandwiches,
    201–202
  Mama's Guacamole, 74
  Orzo and Sundried Tomato Salad, 79
  So-Easy-It's-Sinful Rice and Bean Bowls, 84
  Southwest Sweet Potato Cakes and Black Bean
    Salsa Fresca, 115
onions, sweet
  Creamy Lemon Comfort Rice, 16
  Minestrone Soup with Ditalini, 175
  Mom's Cure-All Chicken Noodle Soup, 19
  Rinkle's Risotto, 156
  The Ultimate Chicken Broth, 19
onions, white
  Baby's Eviction Notice Pineapple Teriyaki Chicken
    Stir-Fry, 64
  Baked Eggs Brunch for the Sleep Deprived, 172
  Fork-Free Turkey and Mushroom Hand Pies, 60
  Impressively Easy Rolled Hanger Steak with Goat
    Cheese and Spinach, 213

onions, yellow
  4 Bean Vegetarian Chili, 183
  Butternut Squash and Chickpea Curry in a Hurry,
    190
  Carrot Cumin Soup, 111
  Freeze-by-the-Batch Tomato Sauce, 51
  Tender Turkey Meatloaf, 194
orzo, for Orzo and Sundried Tomato Salad, 79

pantry items, 67
Parmesan cheese
  3 Cheese Chile Cornbread, 184
  40-Weeks-and-Counting Spicy Eggplant Parme-
    san, 63
  Cloudy Day Meatballs, 185–186
  Creamy Curry Chicken Penne, 210
  Dinner-in-a-Pinch Classic Pesto, 52
  I Can Pretend It's Date Night Gnocchi, 209
  Minestrone Soup with Ditalini, 175
  Mom-to-Be Sausage and Veggie Ziti, 56
  Rinkle's Risotto, 156
  Small Bites Mini Quiche, 171
  Truffle Parmesan Crack Fries, 23
  White Bean, Pumpkin and Kale Puree, 152
pasta, fusilli, for Mom-to-Be Sausage and Veggie
  Ziti, 56
pasta, ditalini, for Minestrone Soup with Ditalini, 175
pasta, linguine, for One-Pot Shrimp and Creamy
    Peanut Noodles with Hidden Veggies, 206
pasta, rotini, for Grab-and-Go Green Pasta Salad, 80
pasta, star, for Winner Winner Chicken Dinner, 160
pasta, penne
  Butternut Squash Mac 'n' Cheese, 107
  Creamy Curry Chicken Penne, 210
peanut butter
  Cut the Carbs Chicken Lettuce Wraps, 176
  I ♥ Peanut Butter Chicken Skewers, 24
  Mommy and Me Green Smoothies, 168
  One-Pot Shrimp and Creamy Peanut Noodles with
    Hidden Veggies, 206
peanuts
  Cut the Carbs Chicken Lettuce Wraps, 176
  One-Pot Shrimp and Creamy Peanut Noodles with
    Hidden Veggies, 206
pears
  Pear and Oat Smoothie, 103
  Pear, Kiwi and Spinach Puree, 128
  Pear Puree, 100
peas, frozen
  Little Shepherd's Pie, 163
  Mom's Cure-All Chicken Noodle Soup, 19
  Munchkin's Fried Rice, 155
  Pea, Potato and Leek Puree, 136
peas, snow, for One-Pot Shrimp and Creamy Peanut
    Noodles with Hidden Veggies, 206
peas, sugar snap, for Goddess Dressing with
    Crudités, 70
peas, sweet
  Grab-and-Go Green Pasta Salad, 80
  Pea, Potato and Leek Soup, 139
  Rinkle's Risotto, 156
  Winner Winner Chicken Dinner, 160
pepper jack cheese, for It's OK Not to Share Jerk
    Chicken Sandwiches, 201
pepperoni, for Baby Needs Pizza Home-Baked
    Remedy, 27
pesto
  Dinner-in-a-Pinch Classic Pesto, 52
  Grab-and-Go Green Pasta Salad, 80
pineapple, for Baby's Eviction Notice Pineapple
    Teriyaki Chicken Stir-Fry, 64

pine nuts, for Dinner-in-a-Pinch Classic Pesto, 52
pink beans, for 4 Bean Vegetarian Chili, 183
potatoes
    Full-Term Twice-Baked Potatoes, 28
    Little Shepherd's Pie, 163
    Pea, Potato and Leek Puree, 136
    Pea, Potato and Leek Soup, 139
    Truffle Parmesan Crack Fries, 23
pumpkin
    Pumpkin, Apple and Carrot Puree, 131
    White Bean, Pumpkin and Kale Puree, 152
pumpkin seeds, for Carrot Cumin Soup, 111

queso fresco, for 3 Cheese Chile Cornbread, 184
quinoa, for Black Bean and Quinoa Burgers, 59

radishes, for Goddess Dressing with Crudités, 70
ramen noodles, for Sinfully Succulent Skirt Steak and
    Mango Salad, 198
raspberries, for Very Berry Puree, 132
rice
    Baby's Eviction Notice Pineapple Teriyaki Chicken
        Stir-Fry, 64
    Banana Rice Pudding, 151
    Butternut Squash and Chickpea Curry in a
        Hurry, 190
    Creamed Corn and Chicken Casserole, 140
    Creamy Lemon Comfort Rice, 16
    Freezer-Friendly Chicken Chile Enchiladas, 55
    Munchkin's Fried Rice, 155
    Rinkle's Risotto, 156
    So-Easy-It's-Sinful Rice and Bean Bowls, 84
    White Bean, Pumpkin and Kale Puree, 152
ricotta cheese, for I Can Pretend It's Date Night
    Gnocchi, 209

safety
    allergies, 142
    babyproofing, 165
    Clean 15 foods, 120
    Dirty Dozen foods, 120
    foods to avoid, 38
    foods to limit, 39
    gestational diabetes mellitus, 41
    infant foods, 94
    kitchen safety, 40
salmon, for Salmon and Sweet Potato Puree, 159
salsa
    4 Bean Vegetarian Chili, 183
    Fork-Free Turkey and Mushroom Hand Pies, 60
    Freezer-Friendly Chicken Chile Enchiladas, 55
    Home-Style Salsa, 75
    Mama's Guacamole, 74
    So-Easy-It's-Sinful Rice and Bean Bowls, 84
    Southwest Sweet Potato Cakes and Black Bean
        Salsa Fresca, 115
shallots, for Heart-Healthy Mussels, 189
shrimp, for One-Pot Shrimp and Creamy Peanut
    Noodles with Hidden Veggies, 206
snow peas, for One-Pot Shrimp and Creamy Peanut
    Noodles with Hidden Veggies, 206
soba noodles
    Quick-Fix Tofu and Kale Stir-Fry, 83
    Soba Noodle and Broccoli Rabe Buddha Bowl, 87
spinach
    Baby Guacamole, 124
    Butternut Squash and Chickpea Curry in a Hurry,
        190
    Everything-but-the-Kitchen-Sink Frittata, 193
    Impressively Easy Rolled Hanger Steak with Goat
        Cheese and Spinach, 213

Mommy and Me Green Smoothies, 168
Mom-to-Be Sausage and Veggie Ziti, 56
Pear, Kiwi and Spinach Puree, 128
squash
    Butternut Squash and Chickpea Curry in a
        Hurry, 190
    Butternut Squash Mac 'n' Cheese, 107
    Butternut Squash Puree, 104
    Munchkin's Fried Rice, 155
strawberries
    Strawberry "Margarita" for Mamas, 35
    Very Berry Puree, 132
sugar snap peas, for Goddess Dressing with
    Crudités, 70
sunflower seeds, for Home-Baked Granola, 44
sweet potatoes
    Apple, Sweet Potato and Corn Puree, 127
    Mom's Cure-All Chicken Noodle Soup, 19
    Salmon and Sweet Potato Puree, 159
    Southwest Sweet Potato Cakes and Black Bean
        Salsa Fresca, 115
    Sweet Potato Puree, 112
    The Ultimate Chicken Broth, 19

tahini
    Chicken Pita Sandwiches, 179
    Soba Noodle and Broccoli Rabe Buddha Bowl, 87
    Yogurt Tahini Dip, 179
tea, for Baby Shower "Sangria," 36
tips and tricks
    allergies, 142
    babyproofing, 165
    breastfeeding, 88–89
    constipation, 146–147
    dairy, introduction of, 146
    delivery myths, 66
    diarrhea, 146
    finger foods for travel, 164–165
    first foods, 92–95
    food safety, 40, 94
    foods to avoid, 38
    foods to limit, 39
    gestational diabetes mellitus, 41
    mealtime, 121
    meat textures, 164
    pantry items, 67
    pesticides, 120
    picky eaters, 142–143
    portion sizes, 121
    probiotics, 147
    solid foods, 93, 94–95
    stop-and-go foods, 146–147
    third-trimester date ideas, 66
    travel foods, 164–165
tofu, for Quick-Fix Tofu and Kale Stir-Fry, 83
tomatillos, for Home-Style Salsa, 75
tomatoes, cherry, for Goddess Dressing with
    Crudités, 70
tomatoes, diced
    4 Bean Vegetarian Chili, 183
    It's OK Not to Share Jerk Chicken Sandwiches,
        201–202
    Mama's Guacamole, 74
    Minestrone Soup with Ditalini, 175
tomatoes, grape
    Gotta Rehydrate Cucumber Tomato Salad, 76
    Soba Noodle and Broccoli Rabe Buddha Bowl, 87
tomatoes, plum
    Chicken Pita Sandwiches, 179
    Freeze-by-the-Batch Tomato Sauce, 51
    Gotta Rehydrate Cucumber Tomato Salad, 76

So-Easy-It's-Sinful Rice and Bean Bowls, 84
Southwest Sweet Potato Cakes and Black Bean
    Salsa Fresca, 115
tomatoes, sliced, for Brisket Tacos, 218
tomatoes, sun-dried
    Creamy Curry Chicken Penne, 210
    Impressively Easy Rolled Hanger Steak with
        Goat Cheese and Spinach, 213
    Orzo and Sundried Tomato Salad, 79
tomato paste, for Baked Eggs Brunch for the Sleep
    Deprived, 172
tomato sauce
    40-Weeks-and-Counting Spicy Eggplant
        Parmesan, 63
    Baby Needs Pizza Home-Baked Remedy, 27
    Baked Eggs Brunch for the Sleep Deprived, 172
    Cloudy Day Meatballs, 185–187
    Freeze-by-the-Batch Tomato Sauce, 51
    Little Shepherd's Pie, 163
    Mom-to-Be Sausage and Veggie Ziti, 56
tortillas
    Brisket Tacos, 218
    Freezer-Friendly Chicken Chile Enchiladas, 55
    Our Favorite Fish Tacos, 203–205
turkey, ground
    Cloudy Day Meatballs, 185–187
    Fork-Free Turkey and Mushroom Hand Pies, 60
    Little Shepherd's Pie, 163
    Tender Turkey Meatloaf, 194

walnuts
    Dinner-in-a-Pinch Classic Pesto, 52
    I Can Pretend It's Date Night Gnocchi, 209
water chestnuts, for Cut the Carbs Chicken Lettuce
    Wraps, 176
watermelon, for Prego Picnic Chili Lime Fruit Cones,
    31

yogurt
    Baby Guacamole, 124
    Banana Rice Pudding, 151
    Butternut Squash Mac 'n' Cheese, 107
    Calcium-Rich Whipped Feta Dip, 73
    Carrot Cumin Soup, 111
    Chicken Pita Sandwiches, 179
    Creamy Curry Chicken Penne, 210
    Don't-Need-No-Deli-Meat Chicken Salad
        Sandwich, 20
    Goddess Dressing with Crudités, 70
    Our Favorite Fish Tacos, 203–205
    Pea, Potato and Leek Soup, 139
    Pear and Oat Smoothie, 103
    Very Berry Oatmeal Breakfast, 148
    Yogurt Tahini Dip, 179

zucchini
    Bun in the Oven Banana Zucchini Bread, 12
    Goat Cheese and Roasted Veggie Tart, 180–181
    Minestrone Soup with Ditalini, 175
    Mom-to-Be Sausage and Veggie Ziti, 56
    One-Pot Shrimp and Creamy Peanut Noodles
        with Hidden Veggies, 206